The Type of Leader Your Org

RIGHT
COLOR,
WRONG
CULTURE

A LEADERSHIP FABLE

BRYAN LORITTS

MOODY PUBLISHERS
CHICAGO

All Scripture quotations are taken from *The Holy Bible, English Standard Version*. Copyright © 2000, 2001 by Crossway Bibles, a division of Good News Publishers. Used by permission. All rights reserved.

Published in association with the literary agency of Wolgemuth & Associates, Inc.

Edited by Ginger Kolbaba
Interior design: Ragont Design
Cover design: Erik M. Peterson
Cover photo of puzzle pieces copyright © 2010 by Alex Slobodkin/iStock. All rights reserved.
Author photo: Alex Ginsburg Photographics

Library of Congress Cataloging-in-Publication Data

Loritts, Bryan C.
   Right color, wrong culture : the type of leader every organization needs to become multiethnic / Bryan Loritts.
      pages cm
   Summary: "Increasingly, leaders recognize the benefit of multiethnic organizations and are compelled to hire diverse individuals who will help them reflect a new America. In this fable of self-discovery and change, Bryan Loritts explores the central, critical problem leaders often encounter when transitioning their church, business or organization to reflect a multiethnic reality. In Right Color, Wrong Culture you enter into a conversation between individuals who are grappling with changing neighborhoods while struggling to remain relevant within communities growing in diversity. You journey with Gary and Peter as they challenge those around them to reach beyond what is comfortable and restructure their leadership team.Known for his passion to build diversity in organizations, Bryan Loritts equips individuals with the tools necessary to recognize and value the culture that's often hidden behind race and color. This will allow you to identify the right person needed in order for your organizations to become multiethnic. "-- Provided by publisher.

   ISBN 978-0-8024-1173-0 (paperback)
   1. Leadership--United States--Religious aspects--Christianity. 2. Multiculturalism--United States--Religious aspects--Christianity I. Title.
   BV4597.53.L43L67 2014
   253--dc23

2014011334

We hope you enjoy this book from Moody Publishers. Our goal is to provide high-quality, thought-provoking books and products that connect truth to your real needs and challenges. For more information on other books and products written and produced from a biblical perspective, go to www.moodypublishers.com or write to:

Moody Publishers
820 N. LaSalle Boulevard
Chicago, IL 60610

1 3 5 7 9 10 8 6 4 2

Printed in the United States of America

Praise for *Right Color, Wrong Culture*

I deeply believe that the future of churches in America will be more multiethnic—not merely to force it as a way to overcome racism or because it will be a reflection of heaven, but because America has a generation that views race differently and is populating cities by the thousands. They are looking for churches and leadership that will intentionally reflect their geographical and relational reality.

My good friend Bryan is speaking from a place of intentionality in this fable that addresses these issues. I believe he is forging a new path for a new frontier of ministry of which the church hasn't come near to scratching the surface. When he speaks on this issue I listen! You should as well.

—**Eric Mason**, founder and lead pastor of Epiphany Fellowship, Philadelphia, and president, Thriving Ministry

There are few opportunities today that are better to demonstrate the power of the gospel than for people of different races and classes to worship together. *Right Color, Wrong Culture* is an important call to this modern-day sign of the reality of God in our world.

—**David Montague**, president, Memphis Teacher Residency

From the time I moved to St Louis to plant The Journey, I had a great desire to see a church reflect our city ethnically as well as foreshadow heaven where every tongue and tribe will eternally worship. By God's grace He is fulfilling this desire. My big regret is not having access and coaching from Bryan Loritts and his groundbreaking book *Right Color, Wrong Culture* when we started. If you are a ministry leader you need to understand the difference between ethnicity and culture. Bryan helps us with an easy-to-read fable that exposes our misconceptions and empowers us to lead in our multiethnic world.

—**Darrin Patrick**, lead pastor of The Journey, St. Louis, vice president of Acts 29, chaplain to the St. Louis Cardinals, author, *The Dude's Guide to Manhood, Church Planter,* and *Replant.*

To my beloved sons in whom I am well pleased:
Quentin Crawford Loritts, Myles Benavides Loritts,
and Jaden William Loritts

To my parents: Crawford and Karen Loritts,
faithful soldiers of the cross, and a model
of Christ-exalting diversity

To the great people of Fellowship Memphis:
You've given the world a little taste of heaven

Contents

Peter

Peter Williams stood behind the pulpit of the Springdale Community Church and looked out over the sea of faces. He had helped found this church more than a decade ago, and today would be the last time he'd preach to these people he'd come to see as family.

He placed his hands on each side of the pulpit, as he'd done so many times before, and began to speak.

"Friends, today—" He stopped. A lump formed in his throat. No one would describe Peter as an overly emotional man. Words like *insightful, compassionate,* and *catalytic* were more accurate, but not *emotional.* Today was different.

God, you really pulled this off, he thought. The church was trending upward, the vision had been cast, leaders had been raised up and now were poised to be unleashed, and Peter had aspirations of helping other churches and organizations experience the little slice of heaven he had enjoyed over the last twelve years. It was time. But it wasn't easy.

He blinked hard and smiled as he scanned every face

in the crowd. Black. White. Hispanic. Young. Old. All worshiping together. His dream—God's mission—had become a reality.

And it had happened in the most unlikely of places: Birmingham, Alabama—or as some people still referred to it as "Bombingham," where in the spring of 1963, Dr. Martin Luther King Jr. and his army locked horns with city commissioner T. Eugene "Bull" Connor. And where the Sixteenth Street Baptist Church was bombed, killing four little girls, one of whom was decapitated by the blast.

Peter and Springdale Community Church worked hard to redeem the "Bombingham" moniker. They were convinced that if a gospel-centered, disciple-making, multiethnic church could be successfully planted in the depths of the South, in a city once known for its combustible ethnic strife, then no other church in any part of the world would have an excuse not to pursue Christ-exalting diversity. From a handful of hopeful people in a living room to now several thousand blacks and whites, along with a growing group of Hispanics—all members of one church—Birmingham's face was getting a much-needed makeover.

"Friends," he started again. This time his voice was strong and confident as he shared for the last time as their senior pastor what God had laid on his heart.

After the service Peter stood in the receiving line, greeting, hugging, and shaking hands with the tearful people as they made their way out of the sanctuary. People seemed to hang on a little longer this Sunday, as everyone shared how Peter had blessed them, not only with today's sermon but with a decade's full.

Finally, an elderly black woman approached him, put out her weathered hand, and squeezed Peter's hand with a strength that surprised the pastor. He recognized her immediately. She had been the woman sitting near the front who appeared to be more interested in her surroundings than the message he was giving. Throughout his sermon, she had leaned slightly forward, letting her eyes run down the rows of people to her left and right. She even turned around several times. Her actions postured her as someone who had lost something so precious that she had to find it. Peter doubted if this woman had heard one word of his farewell address.

"I grew up in this city," she began, her voice quavering from the weight of so many years. "I was here during segregation. For years I worked as a domestic, cleaning the homes of white folk. I remember when Dr. King came to town and they unleashed those dogs and turned those

9

water hoses on our children. I wept for weeks when they killed those four little girls—and in church no less. I never thought I'd see the day when a black man would lead a congregation of blacks *and* whites in this same town that was filled with so much hate." She shook her head and sniffed quietly. "After all these years of praying for our city, I just had to come and see this church for myself. It's true, it's true. My eyes have seen it. For years, young man, I prayed for someone like you to come." She placed her other hand on Peter's and squeezed just a little harder. "You are the answer to my prayers."

Reaching into her purse, this saint of a woman took out her handkerchief and dabbed at her eyes. As she shuffled toward the door, Peter watched her and smiled. In one conversation this woman not only validated his labors but inspired him to do more. But more what? What would the next season of Peter's life look like?

Part 1

Gary

Chapter 1

"Hey, Peter, ever heard the one about the golfer and the funeral procession?"

Peter had just hit the ball—a beautiful, high-sweeping draw that landed in the middle of the fairway and ran for what seemed like days. Slapping high-five with one of his playing partners, Peter returned the club to his bag.

"No, I haven't, Marcus. But I'm sure you're going to tell me." Marcus was always good for inserting humor into every conversation.

"So this guy walks to his ball on the green, which sits right next to a busy street," Marcus said, clearly relishing his new joke. "He notices a long line of cars with their lights turned on and concludes it's a funeral procession. Homeboy immediately takes his hat off, bows his head in a stunning display of reverence, and waits for the procession to pass by before he putts. Well, his partners are blown away by now, because this is not that kind of dude. You know what I'm saying? Finally, one of his homies says, 'Man, all these years of knowing you, I've never seen you show such respect, such honor. That touched me, man.' Putting his cap back on, he replies, 'We were married thirty-five years; that's the least I could do!'"

Marcus, Peter, and the two others in their foursome—Eddie and Thomas—laughed heartily. Someone from the group behind them coughed loudly, signaling that he thought Peter's group was taking too long to play. Picking up his bag and heading toward the golf cart, Peter said, "Marcus, that's why I love hanging out with you. No matter how stressed I may be, I always walk off the eighteenth fairway in a better mood. I don't know what I'd do without you and your silly jokes!"

Peter was glad he was spending time with Marcus and the guys today. It had been a busy week. To be sure, it had been a busy three years since he'd left Springdale Community to launch The Kainos Group, a consulting firm that helped existing churches transition into more multiethnic congregations. In that brief span of time Peter had built one of the most innovative firms in the church world. And his business was flourishing. A culture that longed for diversity, coupled with relatively few multiethnic churches across the ecclesiological landscape, put The Kainos Group squarely in the crosshairs of many pastors and leaders. If it had not been for his love of golf and these three golfing buddies, Peter could have easily burned out.

"Hey, if you liked that joke, try this one!" Marcus continued. The laughter, fast fairways, and errant shots continued for the next several hours. Pulling up to the final green, Peter checked his phone and realized he had just missed a call, followed by a text message:

Give me a call as soon as you can. Pretty urgent.
Gary Kirkland.

Peter frowned. A call from Gary Kirkland was pretty rare these days, especially one followed by a text. He continued the camaraderie with the guys, but his mind was elsewhere.

Wonder what Gary wants?

When Eddie tapped in the last putt and they all shook hands, Peter made his split. "Gotta run, guys. I have some business to take care of."

"What?" Eddie said. "Can't it wait? What about the grill? We always hang at the grill after golfing."

"No can do this time. Sorry. See you later!"

Peter walked to his car, dropped his golf bag in the trunk, and slid into the driver's seat. Then he pulled out his phone and dialed Gary's number.

"Let me guess. You were on the golf course," Gary said,

with a chuckle in his voice, as soon as he answered.

"You know me so well."

"Gotten better?"

"No. I feel like Sisyphus. Always pushing that rock up the hill. Just when I think my golf game has arrived, it goes downhill again. Got your call and your text. I'm guessing you weren't checking on my handicap. What's up?"

"Well, I've got some great and challenging stuff happening here at the church."

"I wouldn't expect anything less of you."

"Thanks, Peter. We're facing some pretty pressing decisions that will affect the trajectory of this church for years to come. They're big enough that I need you to spend some time on the ground with us."

Peter was pleasantly surprised by the invitation. Gary must be shaking things up at his church and needed backup. "You know I'm here to help in any way I can. How soon are we talking?"

"Can you get here next week? I know it's a lot to ask on such short notice." Then as if to offer a reward, Gary said, "Maybe even bring your clubs?"

Peter laughed. "You're speaking my love language. I'm there."

As he hung up the phone, he felt a thrill run through him. His old colleague and mentor had turned to him for help. Unaware of the exact challenges Gary faced, Peter was looking forward to some time with his friend and knew whatever the issue, Gary could count on Peter's support.

Chapter 2

As soon as Peter walked off the airplane and onto the jetway, he felt as if he'd entered a sauna. He tried to take a deep breath, but the air was so heavy it seemed to lodge in his throat. All he wanted to do was get into an air-conditioned area and stay there.

He quickly grabbed his luggage from baggage claim and was just starting to feel cool when the blast of blistering air clutched at him again as he stepped into the Memphis September afternoon. Thankfully, Gary had just driven up to the curb in his silver Prius and jumped out.

"Peter!" Gary said and embraced him tightly. The sweat caused Peter's shirt to cling to his body. "Miss that dry California heat on a day like today, don't you?"

Peter laughed. "Alabama has this heat too, but I just never get used to it." He threw his things in the trunk and slid into the passenger's side. "Ahhhh," he said as he pointed the air-conditioning vents directly toward him.

Gary chuckled. "Hungry?"

They made small talk as Gary drove. Peter glanced out the window at the sights. The aging buildings, impoverished communities, and general grit gave Peter a clear sense of this blue-collar Southern city.

Gary noticed Peter watching the view. "This is an interesting city. When I first moved here, they told me that if you stick around long enough, the city will get to you. There's a grit, a soul to Memphis that sets her apart from the supermodel Southern cities like Atlanta and Nashville. I guess that's why you either hate her or love her. You're either on your way out of Memphis, or you've made a vow of 'til death do us part."

"And how do you feel about it?" Peter asked.

Gary grinned. "Ask me after you've helped us out."

Twenty minutes later, Gary and Peter were seated in a window booth at a Perkins, sipping iced tea, and waiting for their food. Peter sat back and studied his friend. Not much had changed in the two decades since they had first met. Even though Gary hadn't gained any weight, he had lost most of his hair. The lines around his mouth were still etched in what seemed to be a permanent smile. It fit Gary's personality: he was an incurable optimist.

"Feels familiar," Peter finally said. "Like that spot you used to take me to in Pasadena right there on Lake."

"Oh yeah. Co-Co's." Gary's smile became more pronounced. "Those were some great times, Peter. If you hadn't come to Washington Ave., I wouldn't have lasted as long as I did. It was because of you that we were able to make major changes. You do know you were the first African-American pastor we had at that church in its hundred-plus-year history."

Peter laughed. Gary made this statement as though it were the first time he had told Peter. Over the years he must have reminded Peter of his historic hiring scores of times. Maybe Gary was losing more than just his hair.

"You were pretty crazy, Gary. Remember you had me team teach a series on spiritual gifts? You called me in your office for our weekly meeting to go over the coming week's sermon and the topic was speaking in tongues. Here I was, twenty-six years old, and I walked in your office like, *I wonder what his take on this is going to be? What angle is he going to preach this controversial topic?* I figured you'd do the whole cessationist thing—you know, give the view that tongues no longer exist. But when I sat in your office you said, 'I hope you're ready to teach the whole thing this Sunday?' Blew me away. I must've asked you a dozen times if you were sure. I don't even know if you knew what I believed before I got up there!"

Gary leaned back and let out a big laugh. An elderly man in the booth behind him turned around.

"I've often wondered why you did that."

The waitress arrived with their lunch. "Everthin' looking good, ya'll?"

"Oh, come on, Peter. You know why. I wanted to see how you'd handle the pressure."

Peter couldn't stop from laughing. "You aren't going to ask me to preach on that topic *again*, are you?"

Chapter 3

During their meal, as Gary and Peter got caught up on family, Peter's mind went back to those three years he spent at Washington Avenue Church in Pasadena, California, under Gary's tutelage. At twenty-six, he had arrived much the same way Jonah finally entered Nineveh: kicking and screaming. Trained in a conservative, white Bible college and seminary, Peter had experienced ethnic ignorance and insensitivity. On more than one occasion Peter had questioned why his ethnicity was not represented in the readings or the examples that his professors used. On campus Peter had often thought of Ralph Ellison's protagonist in his book *Invisible Man*. Ellison, in a stroke of literary genius, decided not to give his lead character—a black man navigating the injustices of Jim Crow—a name. It was the inhumanity of ambiguity that identified many readers with Ellison's *Invisible Man*, and Peter felt this same ambiguity as he traversed the halls of Bible college and seminary. Where were the people of color as the professors stated examples of great preachers and theological minds? Why did hardly any of the chapel speakers look like Peter? And why did it seem that it was only he and the other handful of minorities who seemed to notice these glaring omissions? These were questions Peter raised often as he settled into this new world.

He would have left the institution, but it was highly regarded and he knew he would be guaranteed a job after graduation, so he decided to stick it out. But after a while he stopped asking questions and simply slid into the numbness of his realization that he *was* Ellison's *Invisible Man*. And so, come graduation day, Peter jumped into his car with diploma in hand, vowing never to become a minority again. For the next year he made good on his promise as he served on the staff of an African-American church. And then Gary Kirkland entered his life.

Dr. Gary Kirkland was senior pastor of the large, historic, all-white Washington Avenue Church in Pasadena, California. He heard about Peter through a professor and contacted him about coming on staff at Gary's church.

Peter had been raised to follow God's lead no matter how uncomfortable—he'd stuck it out at the school and seminary, after all—but he wasn't interested in Gary's offer. He was comfortable. He was with his own people. Washington Avenue could find another poster boy for a white church trying to look multiethnic. But God wouldn't drop the matter, and the more Peter refused, the more God pulled at his mind, until finally during yet another sleepless night, Peter gave in to what he knew was God's will. Peter submitted to God with his body but not with his heart. This was *not* the way things were supposed to turn out.

So Peter accepted Gary's invitation, and on a hot day in July in the late 1990s, Peter began his tenure at Washington Avenue Church.

Okay, Lord, Peter prayed. *You know I don't like it here, but I'm here. So whenever you want to move me, I'm game.*

A few weeks later Peter preached his first sermon, and the response to this twenty-six-year-old black pastor—the first in the church's one-hundred-plus-year history—was overwhelming, even to Peter. The parishioners couldn't stop talking about how gifted a communicator he was, and how refreshing it was to hear the insight of this young man as he spoke from God's Word.

Less than a month later, Gary called Peter into his office and explained, "For years, Washington Avenue's survival has been contingent upon her embracing the new multiethnic realities surrounding the church. White flight is not the answer. With more African Americans, Hispanics, and Asians moving into the community, our church *has* to change. It's a bold move. And I think you're the one to help us do just that."

Peter immediately felt suspicious. Did Gary know what he was getting into? And why had God placed Peter there to help? Didn't God know that Peter wasn't really into the multiethnic scene?

"The pulpit is the steering wheel of the church," Gary continued, "so I'd like to plan a series in which you and I team teach. We'll focus on spiritual gifts." Peter was excited about getting to preach, but then had second thoughts when the week on speaking in tongues came and he discovered that he would handle the entire message. When Peter pressed Gary for his position on the subject, his friend refused to answer, and Peter felt as if he were being set up as a fall guy.

As the series progressed, more and more people shared their excitement about the preaching. The team teaching model was working. Peter not only had great communication skills and strong theological content, but his years in white Bible college and seminary had taught him how to communicate with the people who filled the pews at Washington Avenue. While Peter preached he would often glance down at the front row where he couldn't help but notice Gary's trademark reassuring smile. Peter felt overwhelmed that this middle-aged, white man seemed to genuinely love and respect him.

The next three years saw a significant change at the church. Peter's consistent pulpit presence impressed upon visitors yearning for a multiethnic experience that Gary and the church's leadership were for real. The church was becoming more and more diverse.

God was working in Peter's heart too. Through relationships with these caring and sensitive white brothers and sisters, Peter found the jagged edges of his suspicion slowly buffing off. He was learning to love and trust. He was no longer Ellison's *Invisible Man*. Peter had a name, an identity that was valued and embraced. He began to settle into his role in this church family. He met and fell in love with a beautiful non-African-American woman, Tiffany, and married her. And he realized how much God had changed him for the better because he'd said yes to this multiethnic "experiment."

Not long after his three-year church anniversary, Peter began to sense that God was calling him to leave Washington Ave. At one time he would have jumped at that opportunity, but now he felt bittersweet about it. These folks were his family; he genuinely loved them. But the idea God placed in his heart was too exciting to miss. So after struggling and praying intensely over it, he walked into Gary's office one afternoon and gave Gary the news: he was leaving.

And he wanted to take some families with him. After they discussed more about what Peter had been discerning from God, Gary gave Peter his smile and his blessing. And six months later, Peter and a dozen families from Washington Avenue moved to Birmingham, Alabama, and planted a multiethnic congregation in the heart of the South. Their dream became Springdale Community Church.

"And so I'm thinking about leaving the pastorate and trying out for the Memphis Redbirds baseball team. I know I'm in my sixties, but what do you think?"

Peter zoned back in to what Gary was saying and found Gary leaning back in his seat, smiling, and staring at him.

"What?" Peter asked.

"You were a million miles away, my friend. What were you thinking about?"

Peter relaxed and smiled back. "Our years together at Washington Ave. You know, Gary, if it wasn't for you and our time together in California, I never would've gone to Birmingham to plant a multiethnic church."

Gary set his fork down. "And if it wasn't for you, Peter, I wouldn't try what I'm about to try here in Memphis."

Chapter 4

I guess you should know a bit about Poplar Bible."

Peter looked across the busy street at the church Gary had pointed out when they first arrived. Gary had become its senior pastor eight years earlier.

"First some history. Poplar Bible was started by two Dallas Seminary grads in 1970. That date's pretty important because, as the world knows, just two years before, Dr. King was assassinated here in Memphis. It's one of the things the locals hate even to this day. It just feels as if the world has taken a picture of this city and dated it April 4, 1968, and won't let us move past it."

Although the King assassination had happened before he was born, Peter was familiar with the details, since it had been such a stain on the country and a hard hit to the civil rights movement.

"Well, in the aftermath of Dr. King's death, riots ensued, a curfew was instituted, and a whole bunch of bad stuff happened. What's worse, in my estimation, is that the churches here never came together as one, and instead drifted further apart. They really missed a great opportunity. Memphis is what I call 'Churchville USA.' It's a hub for a major white denomination, but it's also a major hub for a large African-American denomination. So you have all these white churches and African-American churches and they never connect."

The waitress stopped by and asked if she could get them anything else.

"I'll have some coffee," Peter said.

Gary raised two fingers and nodded at the waitress.

"Back to Poplar. So these Dallas grads thought the problem with whites and blacks coming together was the whole denominational thing. African Americans weren't going to attend a white denomination for sure, and whites were as likely to attend the black denomination as you would be attending a Klan rally."

Peter exhaled softly.

"But they thought that if they took the denominational labels off and just planted a Bible-teaching church, they would be able to appeal to a broader audience."

"So these two men tried to plant a multiethnic church?"

"Not sure," Gary said. "Remember the year was 1970, and as naïve and ambitious as these two men were, they didn't realize they were walking into the tension surrounding public school integration. Now admittedly, that had begun to happen earlier in the 1960s, but the whole Dr. King thing had everyone freaking out here. I mean there was some real fear among whites. So the white Christian community in Memphis responded by starting their own private schools. They figured if they couldn't legally keep schools segregated, they would create their own private 'Christian' schools and price the 'undesirables' out."

Gary lifted his fingers into quotation marks when he said *Christian* and *undesirables*. Then he looked uncharacteristically frustrated. "Think about that for a minute, Peter. Christians starting their own schools as a form of protest against diversity and integration." He shook his head.

"Same was true for Birmingham, and most cities in the South," Peter responded. "So what happened?"

"Look across the street."

Peter peered out the window. It was about 2:30, and a long line of cars was beginning to form, with parents waiting to pick up their children from school. Peter noticed a sign looming over the school: Poplar Christian Academy.

The waitress reappeared with two cups and a pot of coffee. She poured each cup full and dropped several creams on the table, along with the check. "Here ya'll are. Let me know if you need anythin' else, okay?"

Peter thanked her and the two men doctored their coffees with cream and sugar.

"So these two men who founded the church were great leaders," Gary continued. "One of them, Lloyd McClellan, was a phenomenal preacher, and under his ministry a crowd quickly gathered. Actually, their growth was unprecedented. White people showed up from all over the city. I think people were looking for something fresh, and Poplar Bible offered it. The Bible-church movement was just beginning, as you know. So the church grew right in the middle of the education and race crisis, and soon the cries for Poplar Bible to start their own school began to emerge. Here's where I credit the founders. They sniffed out right away the racism that was driving this, and they resisted. Man, these guys were ahead of their time." Gary paused and smiled, obviously impressed with the church's founders. "Well, a big church political fight began. An elder board meeting was called, and the founders were promptly voted down, and then out."

"They fired them?" Peter asked.

Gary nodded. "Unfortunately. That was 1972. Later on that same year Poplar Christian Academy was started, and like the church, it grew really fast."

Peter had heard versions of this same tale many times through the years, never growing numb to the story.

Sitting with Gary and listening to him talk while he watched the line of cars grow, Peter felt a combination of sadness, anger, and hope. Was there anything he could do to help his mentor and friend right the wrongs of the past?

"I don't want to make this too long, Peter, but it's important I tell you a little bit more about Poplar Bible Church and Poplar Christian Academy, so you'll know how to help us. 'Hang in there,' I heard a young preacher say years ago in Pasadena, 'I'm coming to your neighborhood.'"

The two shared a laugh as Gary mimicked the words that Peter would (and still) say in his sermons when he felt like he was offering a long explanation on a particular point in Scripture.

"So the two founders get kicked out, and next came Dr. Lloyd Johns. He was from Alabama—"

"I've heard of him."

"Well, under Dr. Johns the church continued to grow and thrive. Dr. Johns was here for thirty-two years, and as you know, he was a terrific Bible teacher, heard on the radio daily across the country. Even today, four years after his death, you can still hear him on the radio. Well, Dr. Johns was exactly what the board wanted—someone just to preach and teach, while they ran the church and the school. Finally Dr. Johns retired. This time the people wanted someone young and cutting edge, so they hired

Dr. Jason Sanders. Jason was a prodigy in a lot of ways—he came here in his late twenties and continued Poplar's rich tradition of great Bible teaching. Briefly."

Peter raised his eyebrows. "Briefly?"

"Ah, Peter, he made the mistake so many young pastors make—he tried to change too much, too fast, without the relational capital needed."

"What did he try to change?"

"Look out that window," Gary said, taking a sip of his coffee.

"Poplar Christian Academy strikes again?"

Gary nodded. "If you're keeping score, it's Poplar Christian two, pastors zero."

"They fired him?"

"Yep. Last I heard he's on faculty at some Ivy League seminary."

"So who came after Dr. Sanders?"

"You're looking at him." Gary beamed. "They contacted me because I fit what they were looking for. As churches often do, they hire a senior pastor who's the exact opposite of the predecessor, especially if that guy didn't meet their expectations. Jason was young, I'm old."

"Seasoned," Peter interjected.

"Seasoned." Gary smiled.

"So they figured you'd be safe."

"Yes. When I came here I had pastored for more than thirty years, and so they thought they were getting a status quo guy who would put it into cruise control and coast, while they handled the day-to-day affairs of the church and school—just as they had with Dr. Johns. They thought they were getting just a preacher and not a pastor."

"You know, Gary," Peter said as he sipped his coffee, "a wise man once told me that it takes between five and seven years before the pastor *becomes* the pastor. Before that he's just the preacher. How long have you been here?"

"I've taught you well 'young Skywalker,'" Gary said as the two laughed. "I've been here eight years. Long enough to be the pastor, but not too long to be considered status quo."

"Sounds like it's time to make some moves. So get on with it, Gary. Thanks for the history lesson, and enough with all the suspense. What do you have in mind?"

Chapter 5

Gary looked out the window as the students were getting into the cars and pointed his chin toward them. Peter glanced in that direction and was caught off guard: it looked like out of every ten kids, six of them were black. The two men sat in silence, simply peering out the window.

"Not quite what I was expecting," Peter said finally.

"I know, and I love it," Gary said. "Neighborhood's changed, and for the better. A lot of African-American, middle-to-upper-middle class families have moved in. I think we have a real opportunity at Poplar Bible to do what we did in—"

"Pasadena," Peter cut in. "Do you think your board will let you?"

Gary shrugged. Peter knew this was a bold move—and the stakes were high for his friend. If it didn't work, not only would the church suffer, but Gary would join his ousted predecessors.

"That's why you're here, Peter. Poplar Christian Academy, and this is highly confidential, has just voted to move way out east to Lakeland where their quote 'constituency' is moving." Gary lifted his fingers again to make air quote marks. "Which is really code for—"

"White flight."

"White flight," Gary repeated. "They say it's an economic decision, but you and I both know better than that."

"Of course."

"So the church board thinks we should move with the school, especially since the school never split from the church. But—and this was really risky and why I called you here so quickly—I decided to push for a multi-site model of church where we explore—"

"A location out east in Lakeland and maintain the current site here in the heart of Memphis," Peter interrupted, anticipating Gary's vision.

"You got it."

"Masterful. And of course, you plan on making the site here in Memphis multiethnic."

"Yep," Gary said and grinned.

"And for that to happen you need a teaching team, with an African-American teaching pastor who connects with the growing African-American community surrounding the church."

"Yep."

"Let me guess. You want me to help you find this African-American teaching pastor?"

"That's why we pay you the big bucks," Gary said and grabbed the bill from the table.

A thrill surged through Peter as he considered this new possibility. This was the type of thing he lived for. "Okay, Gary, so where do we begin?"

Gary's ever-present smile widened. "Where else? The church chairman. He's not convinced this is the move we need to make." Then Gary turned serious and tapped the bill against the table a few times before he continued. "I'm going to warn you, Peter, you haven't quite encountered anyone like Jackson Rush."

"How so?"

"You know how most people have a filter between their brain and their tongue?"

"Yeah."

"Jackson wasn't born with one."

The thrill Peter had just felt immediately dropped with a thud into his stomach. He inhaled deeply and let it out slowly. "So when do we see him?"

"Tonight."

Part 2

Jackson

Chapter 6

Gary dropped Peter off at the hotel with enough time for Peter to do some research and check in with his wife before they headed out to meet Jackson for dinner. Immediately, Peter went on Poplar Bible's website and clicked on the staff page. In his work as a consultant Peter had learned to ignore the generic audience photos on a church's website, and instead actually see the people who worked on staff. Staff photos don't lie. If a picture tells a thousand words, staff photos tell a whole book about who a church actually is.

Peter exhaled as he scrolled down the page.

Gary really has his work cut out for him, he thought. Outside of the sports director, all of the pastoral and director positions at the church were white. Even the whole elder board was white. No wonder African Americans weren't coming to the church even though the community surrounding Poplar Bible was becoming majority black. Peter understood that in a technology-driven age people no longer need to go to church for a test drive, they can do it right at home behind their computers. Podcasts and staff pictures speak more loudly than plastered vision statements.

Next Peter ventured to the media link on the church's site. Several years before Gary had invited Peter to preach there, but a conflict hadn't allowed Peter to make it. Now Peter wanted to know if Gary had invited any other African-American preachers, or if he was still playing it safe. Something told him that Gary had, and sure enough, after scrolling down he saw a link to a well-known African-American preacher. The title of his message piqued Peter's interests: "Donkeys and Elephants: Would Jesus be Democrat or Republican?" It was dated in October, which was during election season. If his hunch was right, Gary had invited this man in to help the people think biblically about politics. Gary had always preached that the kingdom of heaven was bigger than a political party. As Peter read the responses to this African-American preacher's message, it became clear that many people at the church didn't share Gary's, or the preacher's, sentiments.

Peter had seen enough for now. After putting his clothes away and washing his face, he picked up the phone to check in with his bride.

"You're late," Tiffany said playfully.

"Sorry, sweetheart, Gary and I took much longer at lunch than I expected. He had to give me a context for what's happening with the church."

"How is Gary?"

"You know, outside of a little bit more face to wash, he still looks the same."

The two laughed.

"Well, give him my love, Pete. Don't forget Bryce will be in Memphis tomorrow for a game."

Peter thought of his son Bryce—living the dream of being a professional baseball player. "Yeah, I know. What time do they play?"

"Seven, I think. He called earlier today and seemed bummed. I don't think he's got time to hang with you. Sounds like they're in and out."

"Well, we'll get some time, I'm sure. Tiff, I gotta run. Gary's coming by soon to pick me up for a dinner meeting."

"Okay. Give Gary a hug and kiss for me, and tell him I miss him."

"I'll tell him you miss him, but not too sure about the kissing part."

Tiffany laughed. "You know what I meant. Okay, talk to you tomorrow."

"Tomorrow, babe."

He hung up the phone and turned his thoughts to the

evening's event. *Jackson Rush and the nonexistent self-edit*, he thought and wondered how Jackson would respond to Peter's presence. Then he whispered, "Okay, God, tonight give me the patience, understanding, and discernment to control *my own* self-edit. For Your sake."

Chapter 7

Peter and Gary stepped into the homey-feeling restaurant filled with customers and aromas of the best-smelling barbecue Peter had ever smelled.

"Most of Memphis's barbecue spots are nestled in back alleys or on busy streets near liquor stores," Gary explained as he escorted Peter through the crowded lobby toward the dining area. "The Commissary has the distinction of being one of the only respectable barbecue restaurants that sits right outside the city surrounded by cul-de-sacs and gated communities."

As they stepped into the dining area, Peter felt as if he were in his grandmother's home, where instead of family photos hanging on the walls, photos of celebrities looked down on him. And if he studied them long enough, he was sure he'd see the deep red, dry rub stains spotting the corners of their mouths. Somehow seeing the likes of Isaac Hayes's or Bill Clinton's photos hanging on these walls gave The Commissary street cred. Peter couldn't wait to get some of this world-famous Memphis barbecue on the edges of his mouth as well.

"There he is," Gary said, pointing toward a large, well-dressed man in the back corner, surrounded by a group of men, laughing and talking.

It was impossible not to notice Jackson Rush. Jackson wasn't just sitting at the table, he was holding court. As Gary and Peter made their way toward him, Peter noticed people stopping by Jackson's table to say hello or call out to him as they were coming or going. Peter got the sense that the whole city knew and loved Jackson.

"Hey, Gary and Pete!" Jackson yelled once he caught sight of the men. He stood and waved them over. Jackson was tall, wide, and commanding. He couldn't have been more than forty years old, maybe even younger. Though the extra fifty pounds or so that Jackson was carrying made him look older. The surplus weight gave Jackson an endearing quality. "Say hello to two of my frat brothers, Stanley Wells and Jordan James. Stan and Jordy, this is my pastor, Gary, and his friend Pete."

They exchanged handshakes, with Stanley and Jordan promising to do better the next time on the golf course against Jackson.

"You play golf, Jackson?" Peter asked, unable to hide his passion for the game.

"Absolutely, Pete. You don't mind if I call you Pete, do you?" Before Peter could respond, Jackson continued enthusiastically, "I take it you play the game?"

"Sure do," Peter said as they took their seats.

"Well that settles it, Pete, we'll have to get you out for a round at my club. How long you in town for?"

Gary let loose one of his trademark laughs, leaving Jackson's question suspended in mid-air.

"What's so funny?" Peter asked.

Jackson looked quizzical, then laughed too. "Oh, I get it."

"I think that would be a wonderful opportunity for you to use your influence to finally rid your club of old man Jim Crow," Gary said.

"You can't be serious," Peter said, finally getting it.

"Gary's been on me about this. Technically we do have a black member," Jackson said and paused. "She just happens to live in Atlanta. But anyways, this conversation is turning way too serious, too soon. Hey, Judith, how about a round of sweet teas?"

Jackson began to ask Peter questions about his family and work, and listened intently, seeming to be genuinely interested—in the midst of greeting a constant line of people dropping by the table. Peter had to admit, though, Jackson knew how to win you at hello. As a pastor and consultant, Peter had met a lot of people, but few were as memorable as Jackson. Peter's head was spinning. Was Jackson for real, or was he the typical Southern gentleman who hid behind niceness, the preeminent Southern value?

Once the ribs came, the three men rolled up their sleeves and dug in. Jackson took a bite, thoroughly enjoyed what he'd tasted, then turned to Peter. "I've done some research on your firm, and you guys do great work."

Again, Peter was impressed. "Thanks."

"I feel like Gary has told me a lot about you, but I don't know what you know about me or our city. I figure you need some context if you're going to help us with this new teaching pastor position."

"Absolutely. Gary tells me you're the expert on the city of Memphis."

"Don't know about all that. Our family's just been here, oh, about eight generations," Jackson said, and chuckled.

"Really?" Peter asked, stopping his fork halfway to his mouth.

"Yes, sir. So what do you want to know?"

"Give me the CliffsNotes version."

Through a full rack of ribs and several rounds of tea,

Peter and Gary listened to Jackson navigate them through more than a hundred and seventy-five years of Memphis history. Peter felt sympathy as Jackson talked about the yellow fever pandemic that ripped through Memphis in the 1870s. Up until that point Nashville, Atlanta, and Memphis were in a dead heat for the number one city of the South, with each boasting a population around forty thousand. But when the words *yellow fever* began to be whispered down the streets and through the homes of Memphis, that was enough to send twenty-five thousand people running (mostly white)—including his family, who moved with some cousins until the illness had passed. Of the fifteen thousand who remained, thirteen thousand died, leaving the city no choice but to lose her charter to the plague.

Over time the city nursed itself back to health, and leading the way was the African-American community. As with most outbreaks, black folk didn't have the means or resources to flee. So they stayed and waited things out. Jackson paused to speculate that the reason he believed the city remained majority African American was because of the yellow fever plague.

"So the face of the city is black, but the pockets of the city are white?" Peter asked.

"You get right to the point, don't you, Pete?" Jackson

said as he waved hello to another one of his friends.

"I guess you could say that."

"There are about five major families here in the city, when we talk about dollars and cents, if you know what I mean. And all of them happen to be white. Four of those families go back as far as mine do."

"That's interesting. Are these families well connected to one another?" Peter asked.

"Absolutely. My great-great-grandfather started the law firm I now run. Shoot, we've done business with these other families. It's because of us that some of these other families are still in business now. Kids go to school together. The whole nine, you know?" He waved to another patron after a man called his name.

"You're a popular guy. Ever run for office, being a lawyer and all?" Peter asked.

"Thought about it, but I'd have no shot, at any level."

"Are you kidding me? I've watched you practically kiss every baby and hug every person in here."

Jackson bellowed out a laugh that couldn't help but be contagious. "I know, right? But look around you, Pete. It's just about all white faces in this room. Memphis is close to 70 percent black." Jackson now turned serious for the first time that evening. "I wouldn't win because I don't agree with the kind of handouts most of them expect. They bite the very hand that feeds the poor."

Peter could tell he'd hit a nerve with Jackson. Common sense, if not the rules of Southern politeness, dictated that he should back off. But Peter had to know exactly where the church chairman stood on these issues in light of the church's upcoming decisions.

"What do you mean 'bites the hand that feeds the poor'?" Peter asked.

"Ain't too much of a middle class here in Memphis, Pete. It's the haves and the 'can I have yours?' It's no secret that Memphis is at the top for our poverty rate. Most of *these* people don't pay taxes. They're more than happy to let hard-working whites pay for them, while they suck off the system with their food stamps and special housing. Man, oh, man, if you're black in this town, you get all kinds of special treats. And it ain't right, it just ain't. I work too hard to give my money to people who don't even want to work. They have babies out of wedlock. They're violent. And lazy. I didn't bust my butt for four years at Ole Miss, burn the midnight oil in law school, and work my way up the law firm to a partner position, only to be forced to share the wealth that seven generations of Rushes have worked so hard to create. They walk around acting like we owe them. *You're* black. Yet *you* obviously worked hard and pulled yourself up by your bootstraps. Too bad your people can't do the same." Wiping the stained edges of his mouth and forcing a smile, Jackson continued. "That's what I mean by 'bites the very hand that feeds the poor.'"

Peter caught Gary's eyes. They pled, *I told you. Let's end this now*. No longer kissing babies and holding court, Jackson was bothered. He shifted uneasily in his chair, and Peter noticed a line of perspiration break out across his forehead. Peter thought of the old line, *When you strike oil stop drilling*. Going for broke, Peter decided to ignore the quip and Gary's silent request and keep drilling. If Peter was going to convince Jackson of the kind of teaching pastor Poplar Bible needed, he had to know the man who had the power to make this delicate decision.

"There's one part in your story about Memphis you left out," Peter said.

"What's that?"

"Poplar Christian Academy."

Chapter 8

"Miss, where's your restroom?" Gary asked nervously.

"Oh, yeah, the school." Jackson shifted again in his chair. "I thought Gary told you about that."

"He did," Peter said. "But he left out talking about the move east. Why the decision to move?"

"Simple economics." Jackson nodded respectfully at Gary. "I'm a big believer that pastors should preach and care for people, and leave the business decisions to those of us who know what we're doing."

"What exactly do you mean?" Peter asked.

"Memphis sits on the Mississippi River, the farthest west you can go in Tennessee. Cross over the Mississippi and you're in West Memphis, Arkansas. So the city limits could only move north, south, or east. For whatever reasons those with money decided to make their way east. First it was Midtown, and then East Memphis, which is a little squirrelly. There are pockets of East Memphis that are still pretty popular—old money sections—but there are other parts that if you're not careful, they'll rob you blind. Then there's out east—that's where the new money goes, to suburbs like Germantown and Collierville. With FedEx being headquartered out there, that's where most of your transplants, what Granddad used to call carpetbaggers, live."

Ever the lawyer, Jackson argued his case well and Peter was beginning to see the bigger picture. Poplar Bible and Poplar Christian Academy sat right on the edge of Midtown and the now not-so-good part of East Memphis. Back in the late '60s and '70s this was the place to be, because to use Jackson's words, this was a "safe neighborhood," and "great community," where everyone knew one another. But with the changing demographics, people continued the age-old Memphis tradition of packing up and caravanning farther east. Peter could see how to Jackson it made perfect business sense to move both the church and the school out east because that's where their "customers" were.

"Pete, I know this ain't spiritual talk, and you and Gary hate hearing this, but never forget that the church is a business too. And since the church and the school are connected at the hip, we've got to do what's best spiritually *and* economically for our constituency, you know what I mean? If I had my way, I'd sell the building and lot to a church that best reflects the face and practices of the community and call it a day—at a reduced price, of course."

"Why not try to stay and reach the changing face of the community?"

"Well, in some ways we are. Old Gary here did a fine job of convincing us to give it a try by turning our Poplar Bible campus into a satellite and hiring a teaching pastor. I've humored him, but I've got serious reservations about this."

"What are they?"

"Can I be blunt, Pete?"

Gary laughed, as if to say Jackson hadn't been so far.

"Absolutely, Jackson, I love your honesty."

Jackson thought for a moment and then asked, "How can I say this? Do you shop at Whole Fresh Foods?"

"Sure do. Love those places."

"Ever seen one in the 'hood?"

"Nope."

"There's a reason for that, and it's all brand driven. These places aren't racist, they just have a particular brand that caters to a particular demographic. Companies get in trouble when they become so focused on being everything to everybody that they lose their unique branding. Poplar Academy and Poplar Bible have a brand that I just don't want us to lose."

Jackson's words hung in the air like the pictures on the

wall, greeted only by thoughtful silence. Peter took a sip of his tea and then decided to launch one more question.

"I know it's getting late, and I want to be respectful of your family, but I've got one more question."

"Oh, I can tell you used to be a preacher," Jackson said laughing.

"Why?"

"Because that's about the second or third time you said you had *one* more question! Gary does that just about every Sunday." Then, sitting up a little straighter, he launched into an impersonation of Gary. "'Give me five more minutes to make my last point.' Fifteen minutes and three points later!"

They all laughed.

"Okay, Jackson, this really is my last question. Promise."

"Fire away."

"I'm intrigued by your branding comments. So what do you think about trying to become a multiethnic church?"

"Ah, yes. I should've known that one was coming. Where do I begin? Okay, so I definitely have an opinion on this."

"Shocking," Gary said sarcastically, but smiled brightly when Jackson looked at him.

"I know, right? Let me first say that I think it's a beautiful idea. And if someone can pull it off, by all means I respect you for that. But it's too hard, especially for an established church like ours. We have a DNA, a brand."

"Which is what?" Peter cut in, already guessing what Jackson would say.

"Let's see, if you're white, highly educated, and make somewhere in the neighborhood of six figures, you'll fit right in," Jackson admitted. "I'm not saying this is right, but it's who we are, and while I'd love to have others be a part of the church, I just don't know if they'd fit in and feel comfortable."

"What do you think it would take to change the church, so that someone who's *not* white, highly educated, and wealthy would fit in?"

"Too much, to be honest," Jackson confessed. "We'd have to change the music, the preaching, and the leadership."

Peter shot another glance at Gary, who was listening intently. "That's pretty insightful of you, Jackson. What about the leadership needs to change?"

"Gary's been nudging us to consider a black man to fill the teaching pastor position."

"I sense you've got some reservations about this," Peter said.

"I think *reservations* is a good word. I just don't know about specifically going after a black man. It feels too much to me like affirmative action, and I've never been a fan of the whole affirmative action thing. Furthermore, I just don't know of any well-educated, substantive, black preachers out there who would line up theologically with our conservative church. From what I hear, most of them are into the prosperity gospel thing and don't do expository preaching—you know, the whole verse-by-verse approach, which has always been the bread and butter of our church."

Gary leaned forward as if to say something, but Peter cut him off. "Jackson, I love you and your honesty. In an age of political correctness, it's refreshing."

"Glad to hear it. It drives Gary crazy sometimes, doesn't it, Pastor?"

"Only in the best way, Jackson," Gary said and placed his napkin on the table. Their waitress came over to let them know it was closing time. Jackson handed her a hundred-dollar bill.

"Here you go," Jackson told her. "No change."

"Thank you, Jackson," the waitress said, picked up a few of their empty glasses, and walked away.

Peter looked at Jackson. "Jackson," he said, "do you have any African-American friends? True friends, not people you just run into at places like this?"

Jackson thought for a moment and confessed that he

didn't.

"That could be part of the problem, Jackson. Maybe if you got a little more intentional with who you spent your time with you'd come to see things differently. Well qualified, African-American preachers who are committed to preaching the Word and leading the people well are out there, we just have to go get them, and that's what my firm specializes in."

"I know. Gary sent me a list of potential candidates, with their resumes and links to their messages. I'm just still stuck on this whole notion of profiling a specific ethnicity. Plus, if there's one thing I've given my life to, it's to make sure that our church is in the best position to succeed and flourish. Guys like Gary have been huge in keeping the momentum going, and under Gary some great things have happened. I just don't want to bring the wrong guy in who will disrupt what's happening, and even more so, I don't want to put the new guy in a position to fail."

The lights on one side of the restaurant went out, sending their table a clear message, so the three men got up, and headed for the door.

"You like baseball, Jackson?"

"Sure do! America's pastime."

"What if you and I catch the Redbirds game tomorrow night? You'll be my guest. I have a special connection with one of the other team's players. My son."

Jackson smacked his thigh in an excited gesture. "No kidding? That's great! I wouldn't miss it." He held out his hand for Peter to shake it. Then he patted Gary on the back. "I can see why you wanted to bring Pete in, Gary. He's a great guy."

On the drive back to the hotel Gary asked Peter what he thought of Jackson.

"Interesting. He seems like a good man; he's just misinformed on some pretty significant things. I'll keep pressing him, though."

Gary smiled. "This is one of the reasons I knew you'd be perfect to help out our church."

Jackson was an anomaly. His worldview was typical, but his approach was not. Gary had diagnosed him well: the filter between his brain and mouth was nonexistent. If you weren't courageous, Jackson could intimidate you with his brash opinions. There was no coming through the side door with Jackson, only the front would do. But Peter knew Jackson was exactly the kind of person a church wanted as a chairman. "Better to have someone you never had to guess what they were thinking, than to have a person quietly tossing daggers in your back," he thought.

Jackson's worldview wasn't going to change in the course of a week. But Peter did sense a potential openness on Jackson's part to try something new and different—*if* he could see the benefit. Why else would he hold off on selling the Poplar campus to try Gary's "experiment"? And if Jackson was at the table, open to a new ministry paradigm, just maybe he could be sold on a different way of doing and being the church. Now all he had to do was pry open the slightly cracked door to Jackson's worldview a little further. And he had nine innings at a baseball game in which to do it.

Chapter 9

Jackson's bow tie and seersucker suit stood out in a sea of T-shirts (mostly red) and shorts, a clear sign he had come straight to the park from work. By the time Peter sat next to him, Jackson had removed his jacket and torn into a bag of peanuts and a hot dog.

Peter pointed toward first base where his son, Bryce, stood.

"You got a good-looking boy there, Pete. Must look just like his mama!" Jackson laughed, his words slightly muffled by the hot dog he was chewing.

"Now that is the first thing I think we've agreed on since we met," Peter replied with a smile.

"Oh, Pete, we have way more in common than you think."

"I actually think you're right. It's safe to say we love baseball."

"Do you really love baseball, or are you here more for your son?" Jackson asked, staring at Bryce as he stood on first base, holding his mitt, waiting to tag a Redbird out.

"I'm sure it's some of both, but no, I really love baseball. My grandfather actually played briefly in the Negro Leagues."

"Get out of here. Are you serious?" Jackson asked, turning his big body toward Peter.

"Yep. His career was cut short by injury, but for a few years he played with the likes of Satchel Paige and Josh Gibson."

"Really?" Jackson exclaimed, phrasing his surprise in more of a statement than a question.

"You know those names?"

"Okay, I'm officially offended. You think I'm some dumb Southern 'Johnny-come-lately.' Of course I know about old Satch, the pitcher, and the greatest homerun hitter ever to play, Josh Gibson. Josh hit over nine hundred home runs, and died young, way too young. It's a shame he never got his shot in the big leagues."

Peter was suddenly distracted as a Redbird player hit a ground ball and took off toward first base. Bryce immediately put out his mitt and waited for the ball to come to him. Sure enough, he caught the ball, stepped on the base, and ended the inning. Peter clapped loudly, forgetting he was in "enemy territory."

"His great-grandfather would be proud," Peter said, staring proudly at his son.

"Is he still alive?" Jackson probed gently.

"No, died back in the 90s just before Bryce was born."

"Sorry to hear that."

Peter was touched by Jackson's compassion, causing him to wonder where the brash, opinionated man who held court the previous night had ventured off to.

"Thanks, Jackson."

"But hey, if he's a first baseman playing Triple A, he's got to be good."

"He is."

"Did he always want to be a first baseman?"

"Sure did, ever since he read a biography on Jackie Robinson."

"Now, he was a *great* ball player, Pete."

"An even better human being. I think there's a lot we can learn from Jackie, especially with the decisions that are facing your board and the church."

"Why do I feel like I've just walked into something?"

Peter smiled. His lead-in was working.

Chapter 10

"I want to return to something you brought up at The Commissary last night, Jackson," Peter said.

"Yeah, sure." Jackson's voice gave away a tinge of nervousness. "What's on your mind?"

"Affirmative action. All last night I thought through what you said. And don't get me wrong, I totally get it."

"It's just not fair. The playing field has been leveled, thanks to Dr. King and a few others. So we need to move on."

"I see what you're saying with the whole things are fair now. And affirmative action—I hate that phrase by the way—*is* problematic, if it's not seen in its unfortunate historical context."

That seemed to catch Jackson off guard. "What do you mean?"

"Imagine you and I are coaching two football teams that are playing each other. The first half of the game the referees are cheating my team. You're getting every call, while we're getting none. Just when it seems like we're making progress, the refs make some bogus call. Because of this we're never able to move the football, while your team is running up the score. Walking into the locker room at halftime it's fifty to nothing. You all are just cleaning our clocks, thanks to the injustice of the referees. That's pretty much how things were between whites and blacks for the first several hundred years of our nation's history. Whites got all the *calls*, and we were put at a severe deficit in the process."

Jackson threw some popcorn in his mouth and nodded.

"Well, during my halftime speech to my team, you and the referees come in and admit that you've wronged us, and then you promise that starting with the second half, the game will finally be called fairly. What do you think our team is going to say to that? Do you see a problem here?"

"Yes," Jackson admitted. "Even though the game will be called fairly in the second half, the score is still fifty to zero. Which means it's not really fair."

"Bingo. So the question now becomes, how do we make things fair?"

"Easy, reset the scoreboard."

"In an ideal world we act like the first half never happened and we start over, but we really can't do that. Just like we can't act like the first several hundred or so years of racism in our country didn't happen. So the next best thing would be to tilt things a little bit to our side so we can catch up."

Jackson's eyebrows furrowed. Peter knew he wasn't buying the football analogy. Just then something at home plate caught Jackson's attention and he nudged Peter. Bryce dug into the batter's box to await the first pitch. Both men stopped talking and watched anxiously as Bryce fouled off pitch after pitch, unable to connect solidly with the ball. When he wasn't depositing foul balls into the left or right field stands, he was laying off the bad pitches, keeping a watchful eye. Finally, the pitcher got impatient and threw a pitch that nipped the dirt inches away from home plate. Ball four. Bryce trotted down the first base line.

"Nice job," Jackson said, looking toward Bryce. "He's got a good eye."

Peter agreed. He wanted to continue his conversation, but he also wanted to watch his son. So he waited, secretly hoping the inning would end quickly. Two more batters struck out and Bryce, who remained on first base, joined his teammates off the field.

Now was his opportunity to continue. "Let me be straight with you, Jackson. Do you think affirmative action just showed up on the scene a few years ago?"

"Not sure I follow you."

Peter was aware that he was at a baseball game in Memphis talking about a very sensitive subject. Looking around, Peter began to speak in a lowered tone. "Jackson, I'm no racist. I love white people dearly, but I need you to hear me say this. Affirmative action, or whatever you want to call it, was going on with white folk way before the 1980s and 90s." Jackson didn't show he comprehended what Peter was trying to say, so Peter took a different approach. "How old is your law firm?"

"Started in 1883," Jackson said, wiping some of the humidity-induced sweat from his forehead.

"And a Rush has always held the senior partner position?"

"Of course," Jackson said, narrowing his eyes slightly.

"Was there ever an option for a Rush not to be a senior partner?"

"Maybe." Jackson paused and shook his head. "Well, probably not."

Leaning in and speaking in an even lower tone, Peter said, "When did your great grandfather retire from the firm?"

"Around 1912."

"Well, could a black man be considered to take over for him—even one who was clearly qualified?"

"No," Jackson said reluctantly.

"So only a white man could be considered for the job. Sounds like affirmative action to me."

With that, Peter eased back in his seat and shifted his attention back onto the field.

"Jackson!" A man about twenty feet away, walking down the steps, called out and waved. Jackson didn't hear him. His body was at AutoZone Park, but his mind was somewhere else.

Chapter 11

The seventh inning stretch had just ended, and Jackson and Peter returned to their seats after an enthusiastic rendition of "Take Me Out to the Ball Game." Peter had eased off Jackson knowing he had disrupted part of Jackson's worldview. Jackson had assumed that affirmative action was a relatively new practice, invented by a bunch of "liberals." On this night, however, Jackson had been presented with a different way of seeing things, a way that he was still processing. While this was a shift, Peter didn't have time for Jackson to make a verdict on affirmative action; there were bigger things to talk about.

"Is your son a Willie Mays fan?" Jackson asked, pointing down at Bryce.

"No, although we get that question a lot because he wears the same number that Mays wore." He watched Bryce, in his stained, number 24 jersey, run toward first base as the players switched places for the bottom of the inning. "Actually, he wears number 24 in honor of Jackie Robinson."

"Wasn't Robinson's number 42?"

"Yes, but since they retired his number across all of baseball back in the '90s, Bryce honors him by wearing the same numbers, just in a different order, thus the number 24."

"Nice. That biography on Jackie Robinson must have really made an impression on your kid."

"Absolutely. Believe it or not, Jackie's story is pretty relevant not just to ball players, but to Poplar Bible and the academy."

"How so?" Jackson asked.

"Well, it goes back to our affirmative action conversation. If you loosely define affirmative action as intentionally pursuing someone of a different ethnicity to provide them with an opportunity they may not otherwise have had, then that's what Branch Rickey did."

"Rickey was the general manager of the Brooklyn Dodgers back then, wasn't he?"

Peter nodded. "History is pretty clear. Branch wanted blacks in the major leagues."

"Now wait a minute," Jackson cut in, smiling. "I'm confused."

"By what?"

"Is it black or African American?"

Peter threw his head back and laughed. "I could care less, but to be safe you can use African American with people you don't know. Unfortunately, some people are overly-sensitive to that."

"Okay," Jackson exhaled. "So anyway, Branch Rickey . . ."

"Right. So Branch Rickey envisioned a day when blacks would have the unprecedented opportunity to play major league baseball with whites. Look around you. All this is happening today at AutoZone Park because of one man's bold vision and intentional steps."

Jackson and Peter surveyed the men on both teams. They were of all kinds of ethnicities and colors. Branch Rickey truly changed the game, but Peter wasn't finished. He turned excitedly toward Jackson. "Now Branch had the foresight to know that if his vision was going to become real, the first African American he brought up was the most important. What this first black ball player had to embody was two things: competence and the right kind of culture. He had to be able to *produce*. If Jackie didn't perform, if he couldn't hit and was a defensive liability, then the door would be slammed on any possibility for African Americans to come to the big leagues in the foreseeable future. The stakes were that high. Thankfully Jackie did produce. His first year in the big leagues was actually the first time that they had the Rookie of the Year award, and he won it! What was remarkable is that it wasn't until two years later that each league—the National and American—had their own Rookie of the Year award. Which means that Jackie wasn't just the National League Rookie of the Year, he was the Rookie of the Year for all of baseball! He *produced*. He got the job done."

"I get that part of what you're saying, and totally agree," Jackson responded. "But what do you mean by culture?"

"Ah yes," Peter replied, taking a gulp of his drink.

"Okay, and this is amazing to me, but Branch Rickey knew what was coming. This new guy was going to be tormented and called every name but a child of God. He had to be able to take it and respond with humility and grace. But the problem was, how could you find that out, right? I mean a guy's stat sheet isn't going to tell you how he relates to people who are ethnically different from him. So what did Branch do? He did something most organizations and churches today don't even think of when hiring minorities: Branch Rickey, *in the 1940s*, checked to see if Jackie had any experiences with whites, and how he responded. Branch saw that he grew up in Pasadena, California, a very diverse community. He also took note that Jackie played at UCLA with a lot of other white athletes, and served in the military. All of these experiences told Branch Rickey that

Jackie was no novice when it came to whites, or racism. Jackie was competent *and* he had the right culture."

"Pete, I think I'm a pretty bright guy, but I'm still not getting this culture thing," Jackson said, fully engaged in what Peter was saying.

Peter began searching for illustrations. "Well, not everyone of the same ethnicity is of the same culture."

"Still not following you."

"Let me ask you this: if Malcolm X was a baseball player who, let's say, was slightly better statistically than Jackie, do you think it would've been wise for Branch Rickey to hire him over Jackie?"

"Are you kidding me, no!"

"That's what I'm trying to say: the difference between Malcolm and Jackie isn't just personality, it's culture. Branch Rickey was equally concerned about competence *and* culture. I don't care how great Jackie played, if he didn't have the cultural makeup to relate well with his white teammates, and to navigate the hardships coming his way, it would *never* have worked. And who knows, my son might be working some office job today instead of playing first base."

A fly ball headed in their direction, and everyone around them jumped to their feet. When things settled down, Jackson scrunched his face and then turned to Peter.

"I'm not sure I get the connection to our church and

school, though. So far all you've told me is how great it was that Branch made the right hire and baseball is integrated. Which really is a great thing. I feel funny even saying that. Of course it is," Jackson stammered.

"You know what's interesting, Jackson? You would think African Americans would be excited about Jackie being in the big leagues, and they were, but there were many who were surprisingly conflicted about him being called up to Brooklyn."

"How so?"

"Remember the Negro Leagues was a major economic engine in the segregated world of the Jim Crow era, pumping significant dollars into the black community. For years the only two institutions black folk could call their own were the church and the Negro Leagues. That's why people like my grandparents saw Jackie's coming into the Major Leagues as a bittersweet moment. It was sweet for all the obvious reasons, but also bitter because the minute Jackie put on that Brooklyn Dodgers uniform, the hourglass flipped over and time began to run out on the old Negro Leagues. Sure enough, in just a few decades the Negro Leagues vanished."

"Why?"

"Simple. Once Branch and Jackie opened the doors, the Major Leagues jumped headfirst into the sea of the Negro Leagues, catching their biggest and best fish. Willie

Mays, Satchel Paige, Frank Robinson—all the Negro League stars—soon left. And that was that."

"I *never* put that together," Jackson said contemplatively. "But that was ultimately a good thing, wasn't it?"

"Yeah. Sometimes, and you know this, to gain long-term rewards, you have to make short-term sacrifices. We sacrificed an all-black league, something that was ours as a people, for something we can all share as a nation," Peter said and pointed his hand in a sweeping motion around the stadium. "I guess what I'm trying to say is that sometimes the greater mission has to trump what's comfortable. It was really comfortable going to an all-black stadium to see all-black players in an all-black community where you didn't feel the humiliation of seeing 'Whites Only' signs over entrances and restrooms. But once Jackie made the big leagues, if my grandparents wanted to see him play, they did so sitting in a stadium filled with whites and blacks. There was diversity, but diversity came at a cost—they had to see those horrible 'Whites Only' signs in many of the ballparks. But they joyfully embraced the discomfort for the greater vision and mission."

Peter draped his arm over his newfound friend and looked him squarely in the eyes. "Jackson, you don't really know me, and I don't really know you, but I feel in my soul that we've got the chance to do something really beautiful at Poplar Bible. Who knows, maybe it blows up the all-white ballpark, so to speak, that is the sanctuary. If we go down this road there will be some discomfort, but I need *you* to lead us."

Jackson looked down at the ground. "It's a lot to take in, Pete. You make some strong points and have given me a lot to think about, and I can't promise I buy in completely. Besides, I don't even know where to begin," Jackson confessed.

"*I* know," Peter said.

Jackson's eyebrows raised in surprise. "Where do you think we should begin?"

"We begin with *you*. As you said, you're not quite there yet, and we can't begin this process of finding the right candidate for the church until your heart is more open to the possibilities."

"So now what?"

Peter sat silently for a moment, watching the final batter strike out, ending the game. The two stood and stretched. "I'm catching a flight back to Birmingham in the morning. Give me a few days to think. I'll call you."

Peter shook Jackson's hand and glided down the stairs toward the field where his son was waiting for him. When he looked back up at the stands, he saw Jackson sitting silently, taking it all in.

Part 3

Jackson 2

Chapter 12

Jackson's narrative was almost five decades in the making. Peter understood that Jackson was the product of experiences and relationships forging him into the man he was now—just as Peter was. As Peter sat in his office back in Birmingham and considered the next steps, he knew two conversations would not change Jackson into the leader who would take Poplar Bible into this new multiethnic trajectory. Jackson needed to change, but how was that going to happen?

Peter thought about his time at Washington Avenue Church, and later on at Springdale Community. One thing he'd learned was that everyone has a worldview, a lens through which they see and interpret life. In the twenty-first century the difference between whites and minorities was that minorities are constantly aware of their unique ethnic lenses; to his white brothers and sisters, though, most of them did not consciously think of themselves as white. What Peter once thought was racism, he later realized was a naiveté that his friends needed to have exposed.

Peter's questions at The Commissary and later at AutoZone Park were like an audit of Jackson's worldview and heart, pinpointing exactly to Jackson how he viewed the world and others. But Peter recognized self-discovery was not enough. The biblical understanding of the fool is not an ignorant person, rather it is one who fails to act on what he knows. Would Jackson Rush, now having certain things exposed about his worldview, be a fool, or that wise person who was ready to change? Only time would tell, yet as Peter looked out his office window, he knew that he didn't have time. Jackson needed to begin the long road to change quickly.

If Jackson's narrative was forged from experiences and relationships, then real transformation would not come just by reading a book or having a conversation; it could only happen through relationships—first with God, and then with other people. If Jackson Rush was going to be ready to lock arms with Gary and lead the church in a new direction, he had to have relationships with people who didn't look like, act like, or even vote like him.

"Sarah," Peter called to his assistant. "I need you to book me a ticket back to Memphis next week."

A middle-aged white woman walked to Peter's office door and looked quizzically at him. "But you just came from there."

"I know. I've got to catch up with a new friend."

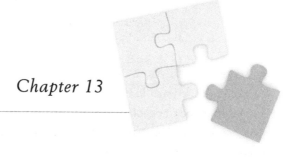

Chapter 13

As Peter stepped outside baggage claim, Jackson Rush was there to pick him up.

"Hi, Jackson," Peter said as he placed his luggage and golf clubs next to Jackson's clubs in the back of Jackson's black Mercedes. "I didn't expect you to pick me up personally. I figured you'd have one of your assistants do that. Thank you."

"Not a problem, Pete. Since you invited yourself to stay at my house, this was the least I could do." He laughed as they got into his car. It smelled new and was pristine. "You really threw me a surprise when you called and said you wanted to come back to Memphis and spend time with me."

"I felt we shared a connection and I wanted to learn more about you."

"Well, Pete, get ready for some Southern hospitality! Now, since you've arrived just before my tee time, I figured we could go straight to the course."

"I like the sound of that."

◇ ◇ ◇

Peter couldn't help but feel as though he'd just stepped onto an antebellum plantation as they entered Jackson's exclusive country club. All the workers were black—from the caddies to the waiters, the cooks to the custodians. It was the twenty-first century, but it felt like the nineteenth.

Just as Peter was placing his golf bag with all the others, an older gentleman called out, "Young man, would you be so kind as to grab my bags out of my car? I'll meet you on the first tee."

Peter looked quizzically at the man, and pointed to himself as if to ask, *Are you talking to me?* Irritated the man pointed to his car, and tossed Peter the keys. Peter caught them in one hand, and looked at Jackson. Wide-eyed, Jackson opened his mouth, then closed it again.

"I'm in a hurry," the man said. "My tee time is in five minutes." He checked his watch and walked toward the men's locker room.

Peter stood for a moment, unsure what to do. A twenty-something black caddie walked over and put his hand out for the keys.

"I'm sorry about that, sir," he said softly, eyeing Peter with surprise. "I'll take care of Mr. Louder's bag."

Peter didn't say anything. His throat had gone dry.

Peter had lost his enthusiasm for the game. This hadn't turned out at all as he'd planned and his golf swing showed it. He felt frustrated, as though his very presence at the club was a betrayal to other African Americans. He was disappointed that his normally loquacious golfing partner had nothing to say and didn't stand up for him. And Peter was angry that he was angry. After all, hadn't he eulogized the easily-offended-with-insensitive-whites part of his life years ago?

Although they made it through the eighteen holes, they didn't connect too well. Peter noticed that Jackson's game seemed off too. Their talk sputtered around sports and trivial matters. And Peter began to wonder if this trip had been a good idea. Finally, they walked off the eighteenth green, loaded up the car, and headed to lunch.

"I'm sorry," Jackson said to Peter as the two sat in a booth at a local diner that was known to serve down-home meat and vegetables—what the locals called a "meat and three."

"For what? You didn't do anything."

"I know, and that's exactly why I need to apologize. That was awful, Pete, what that man did. His assumption that you were one of the workers. I have no clue how you feel exactly, but I'm amazed you didn't rip his head off with your nine iron."

Peter had to lean in to hear Jackson. There was a softness in his voice that Peter assumed was born out of embarrassment. Only knowing Jackson for a matter of days, Peter had never seen this side of him, but what's more is that he didn't even know that he *had* this side. This was a much different Jackson from the one he met holding court at The Commissary.

Over the next several hours in this small Memphis café, Jackson and Peter were proving themselves to be fast friends. Peter talked about the deep hurt of feeling ambiguous as he walked the halls of white conservative institutions. He shared about the pervasive sensation of always having to prove himself when he stood to preach in white churches, knowing they were wondering if he actually had substance to him. And then he shared the fresh wounds of just having a set of car keys tossed to him as if he were the help.

Jackson shared his frustrations too. Why were African Americans so sensitive at times? Why would they vote for a man just because of his skin color? How could he be so naïve as to not see the racism among some members at his club? What did it feel like to be left out simply because of the color of your skin?

At the end of the evening Peter knew that Jackson still had lingering questions, but more important, Jackson had experienced, for just a few moments, the bitter challenges of life in another man's shoes.

Chapter 14

The next day Jackson and Peter walked into an old building, just south of Beale Street, with a bright red sign over it that announced Henry's Fried Chicken.

"Chicken so good it has to be on the menu at the feast of the new covenant," Jackson said proudly.

"Where's the restroom?" Peter asked a server as soon as they entered. The man pointed him toward the back of the restaurant. Moments later Peter emerged wearing a curious look.

"What's up, Pete?" Jackson asked as soon as Peter was next to him.

"That's odd," he said, shaking his head and staring around the room. "Where's the women's room?"

Jackson shrugged. "In all my years of coming here I couldn't tell you. My guess is it's behind the register." He pointed to a much smaller room that ran parallel to the large open area where all of the customers sat in their own heaven eating chicken.

"Hmm," Peter said and began to study some old pictures on the wall. After a few moments, he said, "Ah yes." He pointed behind where Jackson was standing to an old black and white photo of the building. "There it is."

"What?"

"Look at this picture."

Jackson turned and looked, then shrugged his shoulders. "What's the big deal?"

"Look carefully and you'll see a sign."

Just outside of the building, on the side where the small room was that ran parallel to the large room was a sign that read:

COLORED ENTRANCE

Jackson's mouth dropped open.

"This is fascinating," Peter broke in joyfully. "This appears to be an old segregationist building, which makes total sense. That's why the men's bathroom is in one part of the restaurant while the women's restroom is back in that small room. The women's bathroom was the old coloreds' bathroom, while I just went to the old whites-only bathroom."

Jackson ran a hand through his hair and sighed. "I am so sorry for taking you here. Man, I can't win for losing."

"Are you kidding me, Jackson? This is history, and I

couldn't be more thrilled to be here!"

As soon as the two took their seats people began trickling over to say hello to the "mayor of Memphis," as Peter called Jackson. But Jackson wasn't his authentically jovial self. His smile seemed forced, as if he were entertaining extended family members who had stayed a day too long. Finally the waiter came, took their orders, and left.

"What's wrong, Jackson? You seem as if you have something on your mind."

"I don't know. I've grown up in this city. Memphis is all I know, and in a matter of days you've shown me things about this town I've never seen before."

Peter leaned forward and clasped his hands in front of him. "Like what?"

"Well, this restaurant, for example. I bet you I've eaten here over a hundred times, and I never, and I mean *never* picked up on what you just did. A segregationist building? Are you kidding me? It's not that I didn't know segregation existed, it's just . . ." He trailed off and sighed heavily.

"Jackson, it's *okay*," Peter said. "As an outsider to this city, and coming from a completely different worldview, I tend to pick up on things you may not pick up on. I bet if you came to Birmingham, you'd show me a thing or two."

Jackson looked unsure. "Close, Pete, but there's something bigger that I'm starting to piece together." He paused and shook his head. "Your way of seeing the world is so different, and it can be frustrating at times." He shook his head again. "But . . . it's actually pretty cool."

Peter felt the thrill of transformation pass over him, but he wanted to play it casual. "How so?"

"Pete, I'll never walk the grounds of my country club the same again. The best way I can describe it is this. My wife does not drink, at all. Well, I really enjoy the occasional glass of wine. In the early days of our marriage, I'd order a glass and she would pitch a fit, get an attitude, shut down, the whole nine. You follow me?"

"Sure."

"I would get really ticked and think, *If the law says I can have a drink, then my wife should be okay with it*. Well, long story short, we were out one night, and me being the jerk of a young husband I was, I ordered a glass of wine. She got an attitude and I just let her have it. I hit her with all these questions and Bible verses. I made one of the best closing arguments ever—I am a lawyer after all. Well, she ended up winning that night."

"What happened?"

"She told me about coming home as a high school girl, finding her mother passed out from drinking. She shared how her father was an angry drunk, and how alcohol had ruined their marriage. I knew that they drank, but she'd never told me that before. She really opened up about her past and cried and told me that everyone she had ever loved had abused alcohol, and she didn't want to relive that nightmare with me. It's never been an issue since. And what's more, I've never looked at alcohol the same. Her perspective changed me. That's how I've felt these last couple of days with you."

Peter looked intently at Jackson and then smiled widely.

"What?"

"I think you're ready."

"Ready for what?"

Peter smiled again. His new friend was breaking through.

Part 4

Carlton

Chapter 15

The conference room of Poplar Bible exuded quiet dignity. With an understated table and comfortable chairs, it spoke more to the value of getting things done than status. Walking into the room, Peter noticed Gary Kirkland at one end of the table, with Jackson Rush at the other. Between them sat three people whom Peter had never seen before.

It was go time. Peter and Gary had spent more than a month working and praying hard to get to today. Had it been enough?

As soon as Jackson saw Peter, he strode to him, stretching out one hand for a handshake and placing his other hand on Peter's shoulder. "Pete, I want you to meet Wilson James, Janice Richards, and Thoreau Davis," Jackson said.

Peter shook hands with each of them, and then unable to contain himself, he asked, "Does every man from Memphis have a last name as a first name?"

To Peter's relief, everyone laughed.

"Just about," Thoreau answered. "The tradition around

here is that the second son is usually given the mother's maiden name as a first name. That's me—my mother's maiden name is Thoreau."

"What about the oldest boy?" Peter asked.

"Totally the father's call," Thoreau continued.

"Sometimes he's a junior, and other times he's named after, I don't know, one of his dad's frat brothers. Ain't that right, Jackson?"

While Jackson let out his usual roar, Peter took some moments to study the three new people who made up the search committee. If ever there was a poster child for what old money trapped in a young body looked like, it was Thoreau Davis. He looked to be in his twenties, but Peter was sure he was actually in his mid-thirties. He resembled Prince William, but with a full head of hair. With his athletic build and regal demeanor, Peter expected to discover that Thoreau Davis played polo.

Wilson James had to be in his seventies. Donning a coat and tie, along with well-polished shoes, Wilson James had the swag of a former president years removed from office. Everything about him said, *I used to be someone important back in the day*. Looking at Thoreau and Wilson sitting next to each other, Peter thought that this would be Thoreau in forty years.

Janice didn't fit. She looked to be in her mid-fifties and

was hardly the Southern belle who put on makeup to pick up the kids from school. Janice was more thrown together. Jeans and a nice button-down shirt that went untucked communicated an earthiness about her. It wouldn't surprise Peter if Janice had just spent the weekend hiking in the mountains of East Tennessee. As she sat eating fruit, Peter felt most perplexed by her, quietly wondering from the looks of things how she made it onto the committee.

As soon as Peter took his seat next to Gary, Gary officially started the day. "I want to thank you all not only for carving a day out of your packed schedules to help us interview candidates, but also for the valuable leadership you give here at Poplar Bible," he said. "As I've shared before, we're venturing into some uncharted, but necessary, waters, and I'll confess that I feel a mixture of anxiety and excitement."

Gary was the kind of leader people loved being around. His leadership style was understated, at times unnoticeable, but never passive or nonexistent. What endeared people to Gary was his vulnerability. Gary didn't just share facts or opinions, he shared how he felt.

Next Gary turned to Peter. "I also want to thank you, Peter, and your firm for helping us."

Peter nodded.

Gary turned back toward the others. "You've already

taken great strides by opening yourselves and the church to interviewing an African American for our new teaching pastor position, and I applaud you for that. I know that's a major step for our church. Before our first candidate comes in, I'd like to remind us all from the Scriptures *why* we're doing this. One thing I've always appreciated about Poplar Bible is that, true to her name, she's a church rooted in the Scriptures. I've always had complete confidence that if I could convince you it's in the Bible then you'd get after it. With that in mind I want to read from Ephesians 2:11–22."

He opened his Bible and read how through Christ, Jews and Gentiles were no longer separate but were reconciled, that the barriers between them were no longer dividing those who belong to Christ Jesus. He finished the final verse—"In him you also are being built together into a dwelling place for God by the Spirit"—and placed his Bible on the table.

He stood silent for a moment, allowing the passage to sink into his hearers. And then he smiled, as he often did before he began an exciting testament to the power of God's Word.

"If you read the book of Acts, whenever Paul entered a new city to plant a church he always had two requests: first, 'Show me the local synagogue,' and second, 'Take me to where the Gentiles hang out.' The synagogue, of course, was the place where Jews gathered. Paul, being a Jew himself, would walk into the synagogue and begin teaching Jesus to his Jewish brothers. I guess if it were me, or most of us here, we may have gotten so comfortable being around people like us that we'd stay in the synagogue, but not Paul. He didn't get comfortable in the synagogue. After a while he ventured across town to take the good news to the Gentiles. If he was in Ephesus, he went to the hall of Tyrannus—the place where the Gentiles gathered. If he was in Athens, Paul went to Mars Hill and preached Jesus to the Gentiles.

"Now in both locations, Jews and Gentiles came to know Jesus, which would seem to present a serious problem. I mean, after all, the passage I just read to you alludes to the fact that there was a dividing wall of hostility between the Jews and the Gentiles. These two groups hated each other. So what did Paul do? I know if it were us, looking at our history in this country, and even in this church, our ancestors would never have started one church for both of these groups. Instead, they would have planted separate churches—one for the Gentiles and one for the Jews. This is the practical thing to do, isn't it? But what amazes me here is that Paul was no pragmatist, he did the difficult and unprecedented thing. He started one church, and put these two ethnically different and hostile groups together, in one body. In fact, team, you should know that most of the churches the apostle Paul planted were multi-ethnic churches. Just look at the names he mentioned in each of the books he wrote. In Romans he mentioned a guy named Rufus. Rufus was no Jew, he was a Gentile.

"What's more were the headaches Paul had to deal with. Issues like food in Romans 14 and 1 Corinthians 8. If it were an all-Jewish or an all-Gentile congregation, food would be no big deal. What did Gentiles care about eating ribs, right?" Gary pointed to Jackson, who chuckled and nodded. "But if it was a multiethnic church, then food would be a big ticket item. I mean, imagine a Jewish family's surprise when seated at the home of a Gentile family who served ribs for dinner. The norm, and this is important, team, the *norm* in the first-century church was multi-ethnic. Christians in the book of Acts would look at Poplar Bible as being weird because, with a few exceptions, we're an all-white church."

Wilson put a hand to his lips and rubbed across them, deep in thought.

"So why did Paul deal with the headaches that came along with being a multiethnic church?" Gary continued. "The passage we just read tells us. Look at Ephesians 2:14–16 again with me, 'For he himself is our peace, who has made us both one and has broken down in his flesh the dividing wall of hostility by abolishing the law of commandments expressed in ordinances, that he might create in himself one new man in place of the two, so making peace, and might reconcile us both to God in one body through the cross, thereby killing the hostility.'

"Why was Paul so committed to the multiethnic church? Answer: The gospel. See, the gospel is not homogenous, it's eclectic and diverse. The gospel is not just for whites. The gospel is not just for blacks. Jesus died, the Bible tells us, for the *world*."

Gary's eyes were twinkling and his expression became more animated. Beads of sweat were beginning to collect on Gary's forehead. Peter knew Gary was in his element; he lived for helping people see the power of the gospel.

"It's the gospel that blows up old paradigms and invents new ones. We see this in our passage, because this is what Paul meant when he said that the death of Jesus Christ demolished the dividing wall of hostility. Do you know what the dividing wall was? It was the partition in the temple that prevented Gentiles from worshiping God together with Jews. Before Christ, there was *institutionalized segregation* in the temple." On those words Gary tapped the table with authority.

"But once Christ died, a new institution—I like to call it a movement—was established where there would be no room for segregation. It's called the church of Jesus Christ. Jesus and the early church planters envisioned a place where Jews and Gentiles, male and female, slave and free would worship God together as one body, one family. It's this sight of ethnic and economic diversity that unleashed the power of the gospel on the world. In a society that was very class, gender, and ethnicity driven, people had no paradigm to put the church in. Rich and poor, Jew and Gentile, male and female doing life together in one place—people didn't know what to make of this thing called the church. That type of integration just didn't happen!

"But Paul said this was *exactly* what should happen in the church. That's why Paul said in Ephesians 2:15 that Christ died to create in himself 'one new man.'"

Gary picked up his Bible and held it loosely in his hand.

"Now I don't want to get too technical, but the book of Ephesians is written in Greek. The Greek word that Paul used for *new* in our passage is a unique word. The idea behind the word *new* is really the idea of invention, something the world had never seen before. What is Paul referring to? The coming together of Jew and Gentile was as new a thought as the Wright brothers standing before a crowd on the beaches of North Carolina with their little airplane. The coming together of Jew and Gentile was as much of an astounding concept as Henry Ford's Model T. This is the power of the gospel. Again, if you were a first-time visitor to the church of Ephesus and you looked around, your mouth would have hit the floor. Jews and Gentiles worshiping God together? Where else were you going to see that?"

He put the Bible back down and placed both hands on the table as he leaned toward his listeners.

"Jackson, Thoreau, Wilson, Janice, you know what my fear is? My fear is that people wander into our church to visit and they leave going, 'Typical,' or 'Seen it before,' or 'Of course that's what I expected. This is the white church.' I don't want to be typical or normal or usual. We have the chance to give the Memphian something different—a taste of heaven."

Gary paused and looked at each person sitting around the table. "Well, what do you say? Are you ready to take on that kind of biblical call?"

Chapter 16

The thoughtful silence in the room was interrupted when Gary's assistant popped her head around the door and informed the team that the first interviewee had just arrived.

"Thanks, Melinda," Gary said.

"If you could have him wait a few more minutes, there's one more thing we need to cover before we're ready," Peter told her.

Peter stood next to Gary at the head of the table. Resting his hand on his mentor's arm, Peter launched in. "Gary, that was one of the most heartfelt appeals I have ever heard you, or anyone, make."

"Absolutely," Thoreau seconded, as Jackson, Janice, and Wilson nodded.

"Now I know the learning curve here is high, and many of us don't know all of what this means, but as Gary said, your commitment to the Bible should lead you to at least explore this idea of the multiethnic church," Peter said, as

Gary took his seat. "But there's another reason I want to give you as we prepare to engage several candidates today, and that is the sociological reason to become multiethnic.

"It's no secret our country is headed toward a new unprecedented reality. By 2050 for the first time in the history of our nation whites will become the majority minority. Or to phrase it another way, whites will become the minority for the first time since coming here centuries ago."

"Why is that?" Wilson asked suspiciously.

"Plenty of reasons, which I don't have time to fully develop. The growing minority population, specifically among Hispanics, is one reason. Interracial marriage where the children are not classified as whites, but are either identified as other or a minority, is still another answer to your question. But this reality of the minority becoming the majority is already happening in places like California and Texas, and it's totally changing the game."

"How so?" Wilson asked suspiciously again.

Peter smiled. "Well, look at politics. The changing face of America is already having political ramifications. It's well-known that minority communities like Hispanics and blacks identify more with the Democratic party."

"Can I ask you a question?" Thoreau cut in.

"Sure," Peter said.

"Is it black or African American?"

"I got this one," Jackson said and winked at Peter.

"Better to say African American to be safe, but to many African Americans it doesn't matter. Right, Pete?"

"Jackson Rush, are you becoming politically correct?" Janice asked, laughing along with the others.

As the laughter subsided, Peter continued. "But those emerging sociological realities not only affect politics, they also demand how we approach church, and I ultimately believe this is a God thing. Let me explain. Right now there are more than three hundred thousand places of worship in our country. This number doesn't just include Christian churches, but every faith—Muslim, Buddhist, Mormon, and so on. Now if we were to ask which of these worshiping communities are multiethnic and which are not, the latest studies reveal that only 7.5 percent of them are multiethnic."

"Wait a minute, Peter. How exactly do you define a multiethnic worshiping community?" Thoreau asked.

"Ah, great question, Thoreau," Peter responded, impressed with his thoughtfulness.

"Sociologists don't just throw around the term *multiethnic* when it comes to worshiping communities. They do have a benchmark, and it's called the 80/20 rule. What this means is one ethnic group cannot make up more than 80 percent of a church or worshiping community."

"So if we have a hundred people coming, and eighty-five of them are white and fifteen black, we're not multi-ethnic? On the other hand if we've got seventy-nine black people and twenty-one white, then we *are* multiethnic?" Thoreau asked.

"Bingo," Peter responded as he watched the board members taking notes. He could tell that this was brand new to them. Gary's smile was begging Peter not to let up.

"So going back to these three hundred thousand worshiping communities in our country, only 7.5 percent of them meet this 80/20 benchmark for qualifying as multiethnic."

"That's both sad and shocking," Janice said.

"No, we haven't gotten to the sad part yet," Peter said.

"So let's forget about the Muslim and Buddhist communities, and all the other non-Christian faiths, and ask, what about the church of Jesus Christ?"

There was an eager silence in the room.

"That number falls from 7.5 percent to only 2.5 percent of the churches of Jesus Christ qualifying as multiethnic."

Peter heard the collective gasp. Jackson's eyes widened, and Janice shook her head in disgust.

"That *is* pretty sad," Thoreau said.

"No, what's even sadder is that *our* church is not a part

of the 2.5 percent," Janice responded.

Peter couldn't help but notice Jackson tapping his pen on his notepad, deep in thought.

"So, and I'll end with this," Peter said, "on the one hand our nation is furiously trending in a multiethnic trajectory where literally the face of our nation is changing. At the same time the church is 97.5 percent homogenous, which means—"

"If the church doesn't get with it, we will quickly become irrelevant," Janice said.

"Close," Peter said.

Gary spoke up. "The gospel is always relevant, having the power to change lives no matter what the context. Maybe it's the optimist in me, but I think we have an unprecedented opportunity where the church is being forced to get back to her first-century roots, to go back to the days when Jews and Gentiles were doing life together, loving one another, all in the context of the local church."

"God's up to something beautiful," Peter said, looking Wilson in the eyes.

"And Poplar Bible has an opportunity to be a part of this new, well, old thing that God's doing," Gary said, leaning forward in his chair. "If this is going to happen, we've got to have leadership that reflects our values. We can't be multiethnic in the seats, until we're multiethnic around this table. That's what today is about."

Peter nodded. "Nothing of lasting greatness happens apart from great leadership. If we can find the right leader to join us around this table, we'll do more than meet the 80/20 rule."

As Peter sat back down, he looked at the faces of the board. He could see they had heard the truth and were processing it. Now it was time to see if they were really ready to make the change.

Chapter 17

B efore we call in our first candidate, why don't you tell us a little bit about him, Janice, since you know him," Gary said.

Janice put on her glasses, gathered a pile of resumes, and passed them out to the team. "You're about to meet a dear young man named Ronald Wilson. His mother, Renita, and I met in college when she and I pledged the same sorority."

"Janice, I never knew you pledged a black sorority." Jackson said what Peter assumed everyone else was thinking.

"Oh, no. Actually, Renita pledged my sorority, which was quite the scandal at our little Southern school back in the 70s. She was the only black woman to pledge. They weren't going to let her in, but I fought hard for her, and she made it. We've been good friends since then."

"Ah, a little nepotism here, huh?" Thoreau interjected.

"I think once you look at Ronald's resume and talk to

him, you'll see that he's more than qualified to serve as a teaching pastor."

Peter took one of the resumes and scanned it over. Attached to the back of the resume was a photo of his family. Ronald, his wife, and three boys—all neatly dressed, all smiling, they looked friendly and approachable. Ronald's wife intrigued him the most—she wasn't black.

"Well, let's bring him in," Gary said.

The door opened and in walked Ronald Wilson dressed neatly in a dark suit, white, French cuff shirt, and an understated but elegant tie. He took the time to shake each person's hand, look them in the eye, and give a warm hello, saving his most affectionate exchange for Janice. Even though there was only one empty seat around the conference table, Ronald asked where the team would like for him to sit. It was more than obvious to Peter that Ronald Wilson had done this before.

"Your resume looks impressive, Ronald," Gary began. "Graduated from Mississippi Union University, then on to Reformed Theological Seminary, and for the last four years you've been on staff as an associate minister at a large denominational church in Philadelphia. I see you're married and have three young kids."

"Yes, sir."

"Well, those are the facts. Tell us a little bit about your story."

"Not sure where to begin." Ronald looked over to Janice, who offered an encouraging nod. "I'm from here. In fact I went to Poplar Christian Academy."

"Okay, I know exactly who you are." Wilson James piped up, the most excited Peter had seen him. "You went to school with my grandson, Carter James."

Ronald smiled and relaxed a bit. "Yes, sir, I sure did. I still keep in touch with him."

"I'll have to tell Carter I talked to you today," Wilson said happily.

Ronald nodded, then said, "I guess I'll begin with my childhood. Parents have been married, oh, coming up on thirty-five years. My mother's a medical doctor, and Dad is an investment banker with Raymond James. Growing up, they used to call us the Huxtables," Ronald said.

Peter recognized the reference to the hit '80s television sitcom *The Cosby Show*.

"Why did they call you that?" Wilson asked.

"Well, it's no secret the black family is in trouble, with divorce being the norm and all. So the sight of two black parents still together and loving each other kind of put us in this rare category here in Memphis. That's why they called us the Huxtables, I guess. The more I think about it, I don't know, I guess it's sad."

The board members nodded in agreement.

"Why the decision to go to Mississippi Union?" Peter asked. "You know in the black community, that's not a very popular choice historically."

"It's not?" Wilson asked.

"No, sir," Peter said. "Any school that proudly waves the confederate flag, and for years had a rebel as a mascot is not going to be endearing to the black community. I know many of our Southern white brothers and sisters see the confederate flag as a symbol of southern pride, but when you look at things from our side of the street, it stands for slavery and oppression." Peter turned back toward Ronald. "So why Mississippi Union?"

Ronald seemed slightly taken aback by Peter's historical judgment on his school, but then adjusted himself in his chair and smiled. "Yes, sir, I completely understand what you're saying. And I did think long and hard about the decision. I was just looking for something close to home, and academically it's a good school."

"Interesting," Peter responded, easing the word out slowly for effect. "I also find it fascinating that you're a part of the National Church of America."

"I was just about to get to that," Jackson said, looking as though he wanted to get in on the discussion. "Because they have a few theological differences that we don't believe or practice."

"That's not why I brought up the National denomination," Peter explained. "For whatever reason, the National church is not a popular place with black folk. How many African Americans are at your church in Philadelphia?"

Ronald thought for a moment. "About a dozen or so of us in a membership of about three thousand."

"Are you friends with any of them?" Peter asked.

Ronald looked surprised by the question, thought for a moment, and confessed that he was not.

"Any black friends at all?" Peter continued.

Ronald chuckled nervously. "Acquaintances, yes. Friends, not really."

The pace of the interview was moving more quickly than Ronald seemed comfortable with. Peter started shooting out questions about his culture and how comfortable was Ronald with his own people, and it seemed as if the interview was going down a trail that neither Ronald nor the board was expecting.

"It says here that you preach about a dozen times a year at your church," Peter said.

"That's right."

"Ever preach on race relationships?"

"No, sir. Just about every time I preach it's a topic assigned to me by the senior pastor."

"Ever suggest that you all talk about race or diversity?" Peter asked.

"No, sir."

"Why not?"

"The thought never crossed my mind," Ronald confessed.

Peter glanced at the photo again. "I see that your wife is not black."

There was an immediate tension in the room.

"Now Peter, I've got to throw a flag and tell you that's completely out of bounds. What in the world does his wife's ethnicity have to do with this job?" Jackson asked, looking annoyed.

"Calm down, it has nothing to do with the purposes of this job. In fact, you should know *my* wife is not African American." He turned again to Ronald. "I only ask because that makes your three children biracial, and I want to know, what are you doing to intentionally expose your kids to different cultures? Or is that even a value?"

Ronald grabbed a pitcher and poured himself a glass of water. Peter watched Ronald slowly try to steady his trembling hands. Taking a sip, Ronald responded, "I'm not sure what you're getting at, but my wife and I view our main value as doing everything we can to see that our children grow in their relationship with God, and provide the best education and nurturing environment they can have. I could care less if their friends are white, Asian, Hispanic, or African American."

"Well, I think we've got all we need to make a decision," Peter said and stood, extending his hand to Ronald. "Thank you for coming. You should hear something from us soon."

Ronald stayed seated for a moment, looking unsure and confused. Finally he glanced at Janice, whose face was now flushed and her eyes flaring surprise and anger. Collecting his things, Ronald finally stood, thanked everyone, and walked briskly from the room.

"What in the world did you just do?" Janice demanded.

"He definitely seemed like a front runner," Wilson said.

Peter smiled tightly. "If you hire him, I guarantee your church will fail in the first year."

Chapter 18

"What?" Janice said, almost coming out of her chair.

"Now hold on," Thoreau chimed in. "I thought the point was to find an African American to fill this position, and we *like* Ronald. What's the problem?"

"Peter, I don't know where you come from, or even if you consider yourself to be a Christian, but Ronald deserves an apology for the way you treated him! What in the world does Mississippi Union University, the National church, or the fact that his wife isn't African American have to do with how he preaches, or whether he's qualified for this job?" Janice demanded, her voice quavering.

Peter sat thoughtfully in his chair, letting his pen twirl between his fingers like a mini-baton.

"I have to agree with Janice," Wilson said, looking pointedly at Gary. "I came here with a lot of questions about this whole position and the need for it. "But that aside—" he turned his gaze to Peter, "I find your questions to be unethical, which leads me to an even bigger question: should you be here leading us in this search?" Wilson turned in his seat toward Jackson. "Mr. Chairman, I move that we adjourn this meeting, and call off these proceedings given the, dare I say, incompetence of this whole affair."

Jackson paused, letting his eyes drift to Peter and then to Gary, who remained motionless in his chair. After a few moments he said, "Wilson, I do share everyone's surprise at the way in which Pete questioned and conducted himself in this first interview. I say 'surprise' because in the short time I've come to know Pete, this is out of character from what I've experienced. In fact, the Pete I know is very purposeful with his questions. My guess is that Pete is up to something. Before I ask for a second to your motion, Wilson, I think Pete at least deserves an opportunity to respond."

"Jackson, I think a five-minute break is in order," Thoreau said.

"Agreed," Jackson said.

The board members stood quickly and exited the room. Peter knew he had to handle this carefully for them to understand what had just happened.

Chapter 19

Peter was fiddling with his phone when the team started to trickle back into the conference room. Even though the tension had somewhat abated, its aftershocks could still be felt, especially with Janice who struggled to look Peter in the eye.

Peter felt as if he were playing the part of a defense attorney about to make closing arguments at his own trial. Everything seemed to be riding on the next few minutes, not only for Peter but for Poplar Bible. Without saying a word, Peter placed his phone in the middle of the conference room table and hit play. A throaty, robust, baritone voice sang out:

It's not unusual to be loved by anyone . . .

The team shot looks of disbelief at each other.

"Isn't that Tom Jones?" Janice asked.

"Hey, isn't this the song that Carlton used to dance to

on *The Fresh Prince of Bel Air*?" Jackson asked excitedly.

"What do you know about that song?" Thoreau said.

"Are you kidding me?" Jackson said, rising from his seat. Jackson moved to the center of the room and perfectly executed the famous Carlton Banks dance—his body gyrating, face etched with a cheesy smile, and arms swinging in a circular motion.

Soon Thoreau joined Jackson, and they were all laughing. Even Janice cracked a smile at the sight of the two men. As the song ended, Peter felt that perhaps any last vestiges of tension had left the room.

"If you were trying to make us forget about what just happened with Ronald, it didn't work," Janice said, finally locking her eyes in on Peter.

Peter felt the tension return. "Not at all, Janice. Just the opposite in fact. I actually played the song because I want to call our attention *back* to Ronald."

"What does Carlton Banks and a '90s sitcom have to do with a National church pastor?" Thoreau asked.

"Good question, Thoreau. Do you remember much about the show?"

"Of course. I used to watch it when it was first on, then I watched it every day when it moved to syndication. *Love* that show," Thoreau said.

"And don't forget about me," Jackson said. "I loved

that show too. We used to watch it in the frat house all the time."

"Good. Talk to me some about the show—and especially Carlton Banks," Peter said.

"Carlton was always getting picked on by his cousin Will," Jackson said.

"That's right," Peter said, pointing his finger at Jackson for emphasis. "And *why* was Carlton always getting picked on by Will?"

"Because he was short," Wilson said.

Everyone's eyes landed on the senior citizen.

"What?" Wilson said, shrugging his shoulders. "I watched the *Fresh Prince* too."

They all laughed, and for a moment Peter thought Jackson was going to have a heart attack. He coughed, pounded on his chest, and turned red.

"Yes," Peter said, trying to bring the room back on topic.

"Will did pick on Carlton because he was short. But beyond being vertically challenged, Will picked on Carlton for a whole lot of other reasons. Why do you think he did this?"

"I guess because they were so different," Thoreau said.

"How so?" Peter asked, encouraging Thoreau.

"Well, just listen to the theme song. Will's from West Philadelphia, the 'hood, you know. Carlton is not from the hood, he's from Bel Air, has a country club membership, and aspires to go to Princeton."

"Yes," Peter said and hit the table for emphasis. "Keep going, Thoreau. How else are they different?"

"They dress differently. To put it in Memphis terms, Will looks like he comes straight out of South Memphis, while Carlton looks like old money East Memphis."

"Yes!" Peter said, hitting the table again. "Jackson, let me ask *you* a question. Who do you think would be more comfortable at Poplar Bible—Will or Carlton?"

"Is that really a question? Carlton, of course."

"Do you all agree with Jackson?" Peter asked, surveying the room.

Everyone nodded.

"But why?" Peter pressed.

"I guess because he's just like us," Thoreau confessed. "I mean, it's pretty scary the similarities between Carlton and me. We both went to private school—"

"So did Will," Peter interrupted.

"Yeah, but notice that Will wore his blazer inside out when he walked the halls of his private school," Wilson chimed in. Everyone laughed again.

"You have got to stop that," Jackson said jokingly to Wilson.

"Great point, Wilson," Peter said. "Why do you think

the show's producers had him wear his jacket inside out at private school?"

"To show he didn't fit in."

"Pretty important point." Peter turned back to Thoreau. "Go ahead with the comparisons, Thoreau."

"We both have country club memberships. No secret, like Carlton, I have a little bit of money."

"So we're pretty much agreed that Carlton would fit right in here at Poplar Bible. What about Will?"

The team shook their heads.

"Will would have a hard time," Jackson said. "He's loud, comes from a single parent home, and dresses and talks more urban."

"I'm struggling to see the point in all this," Janice said as she crossed her arms. "What do Carlton Banks and Will Smith have to do with Ronald?"

The room fell quiet again as the team waited for Peter's response. Peter looked thoughtfully at each of the board members. He wanted to make sure they understood his sincerity.

"What we've just stumbled onto is a very important topic," he said finally. "One that, sadly, most companies, organizations, and churches don't even consider when it comes to hiring minorities. What *The Fresh Prince of Bel Air* teaches us is that there is a difference between ethnicity and culture. When it comes to building diverse teams, ethnicity is never enough. You can hire the right ethnicity, but the wrong culture. Make this mistake and you will spend a minimum of eighteen months cleaning up your mess. My fear is, we almost did that with Ronald."

Chapter 20

The quiet that hovered over the conference room turned from brooding to reflective.

"I see your point about the difference between ethnicity and culture. This is all eye-opening to me as a white person," Thoreau confessed. "I guess I just don't see myself with any ethnic or cultural lenses, so all this is so new to me."

"Which is why you always need to have someone on your search committee who represents the ethnicity you're trying to hire. If not, you're bound to make some pretty significant mistakes," Peter responded.

"I hear what you're saying," Janice said, her arms still crossed. "But is there any *biblical* basis for this whole ethnicity versus culture thing?"

"Actually it's all over the Bible."

"Really?" Wilson said and leaned forward slightly.

"Absolutely. For example, look at the opening verses of Acts, chapter six."

Gary picked up his Bible and flipped pages until he found the verse. He looked at Wilson and then passed him the Bible. "Wilson, why don't you read verse one for us?"

Wilson took the Bible and adjusted his glasses. He moved a finger down the page until he landed at the verse. "Now in these days when the disciples were increasing in number, a complaint by the Hellenists arose against the Hebrews because their widows were being neglected in the daily distribution." He looked up expectantly.

"The book of Acts presents a history of the early church," Peter said. "By the time we get to this passage, the church was off and running, and here we see the author, Luke, documenting a conflict that arose within her ranks. Notice carefully the terms he used: *Hellenists* and *Hebrews*.

"Luke was clear that there was a clash going on between these two groups. Scholars agree that the Hellenists and Hebrews were both Jews ethnically. So what was Luke getting at when he called some Jews Hellenists and other Jews Hebrews? I'll tell you, Luke was dealing with the issue of culture. Now, as my Sunday school teacher used to say, 'Let's put on our thinking caps.' Talk to me about Hellenism. What is that?"

"The spread of Greek culture," Thoreau said.

"That's right! Alexander the Great was not just interested in acquiring land and kingdoms, he wanted to inject Greek culture everywhere he went. That's why he encouraged his soldiers to settle down, marry foreign women, and have families. It's also why Alexander set up libraries all over the world—he wanted Greece not just to be a place, but to be a culture."

Janice exhaled heavily, but she uncrossed her arms.

"I'm leaving a lot out here, but when Luke talked about the Hellenistic Jews, he was talking about ethnic Jews who embraced Greek culture. They looked Jewish, but acted Greek. They ate non-kosher food, named their kids Greek names, spoke Greek, and adopted Greek practices in how they dressed and where they hung out."

Peter walked to a whiteboard on the far end of the room and picked up a marker from the board's ledge. "Sociologists point out that within every ethnicity exists at least three cultures—with many variations. For our purposes we'll focus on the three main ones. Let's call them C1, C2, and C3."

He noticed the team started to take notes.

That's good, he thought. *They want to learn this*.

"C1s are defined as people within a certain ethnic group who have assimilated into another ethnic group. In the Acts 6 text they were the Hellenists—they were ethnic Jews who assimilated into Greek culture. On *The Fresh*

Prince of Bel Air, Carlton Banks would be your C1."

"Ah, I see," Jackson said, tapping his pen on his notepad. "Carlton is black ethnically, but white culturally."

"Yes!" Peter said.

"On the other extreme are your C3s. These are people within an ethnic group who absolutely refuse to assimilate within other ethnic groups or cultures. C3s tend to be your rage against the machine, 'keep it real,' tribe of people within an ethnic group. They refuse to adjust, or what some would call *contextualize*. In our text those are the Hebrews. Interestingly enough, the apostle Paul actually described himself once as a C3."

"Where does he say that?" Wilson asked in disbelief.

"Philippians 3:5."

Wilson began to turn the Bible's pages.

"Read it out loud when you find it," Peter said.

"Circumcised on the eighth day, of the people of Israel, of the tribe of Benjamin, a Hebrew of Hebrews," Wilson read.

"In this one verse Paul dealt with both his ethnicity and culture. When he said that he was of the 'people of Israel,' he was referring to the fact that he was a Jew—he was pointing to his ethnicity. Ah, but when Paul said that he was a 'Hebrew of Hebrews,' what was he getting at?"

"Culture," Thoreau answered.

"I've read the Bible all my life and have never noticed this," Wilson confessed.

"But what kind of culture was Paul talking about when he said that he was a 'Hebrew of Hebrews'?" Peter asked.

"He was saying he was a C3," Thoreau answered.

"So getting back to the *Fresh Prince* example. If Carlton is a C1, what's Will?" Peter's gaze went from face to face.

"C3," Jackson responded, and rocked back and forth, as if he were impressed with his answer.

"Bingo," Peter said.

"And that's why Carlton and Will are always at it," Wilson said, his face showing comprehension.

"That's right, Wilson. C1s and C3s are always going to clash."

"Is that because C3s are more *black* than C1s?" Jackson asked.

Peter stepped from the whiteboard and returned to the conference table. He took a sip of his water and paused, thinking of a way to respond. "Very interesting question, Jackson," he finally said, and returned his glass to the table.

Jackson's face paled. "I've offended you," he said apologetically. "Forgive me."

124

"You haven't, Jackson, you're okay," Peter assured him. "I guess the trouble with your question is in order to answer, you've got to give me a definition of *black*. What's black? Yo, if I talk like dis, homie, is that black? Or if I use words like *coalesce* or *genuflect*, does that now mean I have to turn in my African-American Express Card? Does that make me less black? What exactly is black? Is it fathering seven babies by seven different women, or is it having seven babies with one woman *after* you've married her and being a committed husband and loving father? What exactly is *black*? Is it dropping out of high school so I can sell dope? Or is it having a PhD? Is black drinking a forty-ounce of Old English 800? Or is black eating a mayonnaise sandwich with a side of cottage cheese?"

Peter could sense the group's discomfort as they were confronted with the prevalent stereotypes. They shifted in their seats and looked down at the table or across the room—anywhere but at Peter.

"I'd love an answer to that question, but since there isn't one, we're forced to conclude that Carlton Banks is just as ethnically black as Will Smith. Larry Elder is just as black as the Reverend Al Sharpton or Ice Cube, and Malcolm X was just as ethnically black as any so-called Uncle Tom."

Peter glanced at Gary, who smiled and nodded encouragingly.

"I'm not making a judgment call here, guys," he continued. "And I for sure am not questioning Carlton's, or for that matter Ronald Wilson's, blackness. That's not the issue. Since we've decided to pursue an African American for this position, ethnicity is not what's at stake here; culture is. And we can't miss it on the culture front. Way too much is on the line."

"I'd still like to know why you were so abrupt with Ronald Wilson," Janice said. "He would fit in well here, and he has the credentials to be a great teaching pastor." Janice was tapping her fingers, impatiently awaiting an answer.

"Gary, why don't you remind us again of what you're envisioning for the position of teaching pastor at this campus," Peter said.

"Sure," Gary said. "I actually don't like the title *teaching pastor* because I feel it limits the role to just preaching and teaching, when it really is so much more than that. This person needs to be a capital 'L' leader, who will work closely with me and our executive team helping to push our body forward. Like anything else when it comes to leadership, he needs to be able to connect deeply with the hearts and lives of the people here in East Memphis."

"Remind me again of the demographics surrounding the church," Peter said.

"It's everything—rich and poor, black and white. Right outside our sanctuary is the collision between affluence and poverty. Some say it's an impossible situation, but you know me; I see it as a hopeful opportunity to get back to our first-century-church-book-of-Acts roots," Gary said, smiling and offering a quick shrug.

"So if I'm hearing you right, Gary, you're looking for a guy who can connect well with black and white, rich and poor?" Peter asked.

"Absolutely."

"Is that what you're hearing, team?"

The team slowly nodded in agreement.

"If that's our understanding, then Ronald for sure wasn't our guy."

Chapter 21

"One of the things that people get stuck on in the hiring process is competency," Peter said. "They look at a person's resume and they see the right schools, the right set of experiences. They check a few references and they're ready to hire the person. Competence isn't enough, there has to be the right culture as well."

"Oh!" Jackson yelled out excitedly and pointed at Peter. "Tell them about the whole Branch Rickey thing."

Peter laughed. He was amazed by how much Jackson had become willing to transform. He held up his hand. "Not just now." Turning his attention back to the team, Peter continued his explanation. "When you hire a person, you don't just hire their competencies, you also hire the sum total of who they are—competence, character, and culture. You don't want to stop with can they *do* the job, but you want to ask, can they *be* what this job needs? That moves us into the culture territory. That's why Al Sharpton will never be elected president. He strikes me as a C3.

Being president necessitates the cultural ability to be able to relate to a broad demographic of people. You've got to work a room filled with wealthy businesspeople, and campaign among the poor. If you take Sharpton out of the black church and off of MSNBC, he's in trouble."

"But using your line of reasoning—and I'm not saying I agree with it," Janice said, "Ronald is no C3. I see him more as a C1."

"Why do you say that?" Peter asked.

"Well, he said he had no black friends and he works at an all-white church where he's comfortable enough not to push the limits. What's more is that he said all of his friends are white."

"You're right, Janice. All of this—his work, schooling, social networks—was right in front of you serving as huge indicator lights pointing to his culture. You all were so in love with what seminary he went to and where he worked that you couldn't see what his resume was pointing to—and that is that Ronald Wilson is your classic C1. He's Carlton Banks."

"Now I'm with Janice on this one," Jackson replied. "Are you saying a Carlton can't work here?"

"Not saying that at all, Jackson. Carlton probably *does* need to work here. In fact, scanning your website I saw that you have an African American as your sports director. He's been here what, seven years? I bet you he's a C1."

The team started to chuckle in agreement.

"All I'm saying, Janice, is that for what this role demands, Ronald is way too safe. Poplar Bible doesn't need another one of you around this table. And that's exactly what you would've gotten with Ronald, just a different skin color." Peter glanced at Jackson and remembered his statement about branding during their first meeting at the barbecue restaurant. "We need to remember that biblically, we should be branded as the church, not as the money or the demographic we feel most comfortable being. That might work for a business, but it doesn't work in God's kingdom."

Jackson took the hint and cleared his throat. But Peter noticed a slight smile cross his lips.

Not sure how Wilson would respond, Peter took a chance and headed to him, where he leaned over and put his arm around him. Wilson simply turned his head to look at Peter straight on. His hazel eyes held an openness, which Peter was sure hadn't always been there.

"You need an African American on this team who will put his arm around you and say, 'Hey, I've noticed the worship isn't really connecting with many in the African-American community. Why don't we make some changes?' You need a go-to guy who will intuitively be able to tell you if that worship leader, or minority candidate, will be a good fit."

"Like you just did when we interviewed Ronald," Jackson spoke up.

"Exactly. But this is a delicate balance. This kind of person has to be comfortable enough in his own skin to work here, but not so comfortable that he becomes another white guy. What I'm getting at is you need a C2, a Denzel Washington."

"C2?" Jackson asked.

"Denzel Washington?" Janice said.

"That will have to wait. I think it's time for our next interview," Peter said checking his watch.

Part 5

Ice Cube

Chapter 22

The door to the conference room opened and in walked a tall, slender, commanding man in his fifties with gray hair at his temples and a kind smile. His appearance went beyond the norm of what the white, affluent East Memphian was accustomed to. His bold, blue suit with the oversized suit coat appeared to be custom-made. His suit's breast pocket had a yellow handkerchief prominently displayed. His shoes matched his suit, and Peter knew immediately the outfit could not be found in any of the stores frequented by the people seated around the table.

"Pastor Mitchell, great seeing you again," Gary said as he stood and embraced him. He then turned to the group, who had also stood. "This is Octavius Mitchell, senior pastor of the Greater Zion Church."

"Always great being with you, Dr. Kirkland," Pastor Mitchell responded and then nodded a greeting to the rest of the group. His eyes moved around the room until they landed on Peter. His eyebrows raised slightly and his smile widened.

"You know Gary?" Jackson asked as he moved forward to shake the candidate's hand.

"Oh yes. Once a month it is my joy to get together with Dr. Kirkland," Pastor Mitchell said.

"Your name is so unique, Oc-ta-vi-us. What does it mean?" Jackson asked, apparently failing to catch the subtle point against using Gary's first name.

"*Eight*." Pastor Mitchell pronounced the number as though he were humoring a child. "I'm the youngest of eight children."

"Nice shoes, Octavius," Janice said as she pointed to Pastor Mitchell's blue shoes, which appeared to be made out of exotic reptile.

Pastor Mitchell appeared uncomfortable but forced a smile.

"I tell you what," Gary jumped in. "I know in our culture it's no big deal to call each other by our first names, but let's refer to our friend as *Pastor*."

"I'm so sorry if I offended you," Janice said quickly.

"No offense taken," Pastor Mitchell said and smiled kindly. "And thank you, Dr. Kirkland, for offering that up. My culture tends to have a different way of addressing and treating their pastors."

Gary pointed to an empty chair, so Dr. Mitchell could have a seat. Then the team sat awkwardly and quietly.

Peter decided to hang back and watch how the team would respond to this new candidate. Jackson picked up Pastor Mitchell's resume and looked it over.

"Pastor Mitchell, I see that you graduated from Morehouse College with a bachelor's in religion," Jackson said.

"Yes, sir, I sure did."

"Isn't Morehouse an all-African-American school?"

Peter smiled inwardly at the question. Jackson was trying to mimic the question Peter had given to Ronald about the racial makeup of his education.

"Yes, it is."

"How does that work, exactly? Are whites allowed to attend schools like Morehouse?" Jackson asked.

Pastor Mitchell gave a hearty laugh. "Of course!" His laugh seemed to ease the mood of the room.

"Forgive my ignorance, Pastor Mitchell, but is it really okay to have an all-black college? It seems segregationist to me," Wilson asked.

"Oh, you're not ignorant at all, and I understand your point. Actually I get that question a lot from white folks. What you may not know is that many historically African-American colleges and universities were funded by whites who were legitimately concerned that African Americans receive a quality education."

"Seriously?" Thoreau jumped in.

"Seriously," Pastor Mitchell replied. "Take Spelman, our African-American sister school, for instance. Do you know whom it's named after?"

When no one answered, Pastor Mitchell explained. "It's named after John Rockefeller's wife. Her maiden name was Spelman. The Rockefellers were the major benefactors of the school. Many of my white brothers and sisters believe that historically African-American colleges and universities began on their own because we didn't want to be a part of their schools, when in fact it was our white brothers and sisters who, out of both a concern for our education and a commitment to institutionalized segregation, funded these schools." He smiled politely again.

"Never knew that," Thoreau replied, shaking his head in wonderment. "But while I see the thinking behind doing this in the 1800s, why does it continue today?"

"Well, because there is still a need to provide rich educational environments where the faculty, staff, and administration reflect and teach our history and values. What other school can I go to that will not only substantively educate me in the African-American experience but do so with professors, a president, and leadership council that look like me?" He nodded his head in respect and chuckled lightly. "I don't think I would've found this at institutions like the University of Tennessee or Ole Miss. Those are great schools, but they didn't soothe the cultural longing *I* had. And most certainly, on a high school level, Poplar Christian Academy would not have scratched that itch, if you'll forgive my bluntness."

Peter smiled to himself. *This is getting good*, he thought.

With each question the committee asked, Pastor Mitchell answered in calm, dignified tones, putting the team at ease. Peter noticed they became so comfortable that they continued to probe deeper into his racial worldview.

Finally they moved to Pastor Mitchell's preaching.

"We've all listened to some of your sermons online, and while I can't speak for the team, I found them to be very inspiring," Jackson said.

"Thank you."

"You seem to end your sermons as if you're very, what's the word I want?"

"*Animated?*" Thoreau offered.

"That's it," Jackson said, pointing in agreement to Thoreau. "It seems as if you're singing at the end of your messages. Is that typical?"

Pastor Mitchell crossed his legs comfortably. "I don't know if I'd say typical. African-American preachers have a very different style from what you're used to. But to your point, in the traditional African-American church many of our preachers tend to be animated, as you say. We have a word for how you describe the way my sermons end: *whooping*."

"Whooping?" Jackson said. "Well—"

Gary coughed lightly. Peter figured he was expressing his concern about Jackson's nonexistent self-edit button.

Not taking the clue, however, Jackson forged ahead. "Well, I guess my question is, do you imagine whooping, as you say, at our church, if you take this position?"

Pastor Mitchell tilted his head and wore a mixture of seriousness and stilted politeness. Peter could tell he wanted to be respectful, but Octavius Mitchell *was* a pastor *and* older than many of the people in the room.

"Well, Mr. Chairman, I've learned years ago that God made only one me, and He expects me to be me. What you see is what you get. Do you anticipate that being a problem?"

Jackson sat up a little straighter, surprised by the reply. "For some it will be. We're not a very emotional church; we tend to be more on the *intellectual* side of things."

Gary turned red at Jackson's misstep. Peter eased back in his chair, twirling the pen between his fingers, now boldly wearing an outward smile.

"Mr. Chairman," Pastor Mitchell stated, still maintaining a polite manner. "Whooping is not anti-intellectual. My sincere hope should be that you learned something about God and His Word in every sermon that I preached."

"Oh yes, I did. I'm not trying to say your sermons aren't intellectual—"

"Allow me to offer an example. From the looks of things, I would imagine you like gravy."

Here it comes, Peter thought. He wondered how Jackson would react to this blatant weight comment. He was surprised when Jackson laughed and patted his stomach.

"You better believe it," Jackson said.

"Well then, you know what my grandmother said is true: great meat always makes great gravy. When the meat of the Bible has been presented, and Christ exalted, good gravy is sure to follow. Do you see what I'm getting at, Mr. Chairman?" Pastor Mitchell was smiling sincerely.

"Got it," Jackson said.

"I believe that it was the Greeks who said that great messages were composed of *logos* and *pathos*—content and passion. Dr. Robert Smith Jr., the great professor at Beeson Divinity says in his book *Doctrine That Dances* that the preacher must be committed to both the cognitive and the cardiological—the head and the heart. Jesus said we are to love God with the totality of our being, head and heart.

The body of my sermons always informs the head, but my conclusions inspire the heart, and that's why I whoop, Mr. Chairman. My whooping gets to the heart—*and* the feet, I guess one could say, causing the people to dance."

"We don't dance much around here," Wilson said. The room erupted in laughter.

"Sure we do. Put that Tom Jones back on, Peter," Thoreau said looking at Jackson. They laughed again.

"I see your point, Pastor," Jackson said, sobering up. "But the cement on Poplar Bible's DNA dried years ago. We are who we are, and to be painfully honest, I'm not sure that your style of preaching would fit. If you were a guest speaker, we would play along, but once the novelty wore off, I'm telling you, our people wouldn't go for it."

"So you want to build a multiethnic church, but I've got to become white to be part of it?" Pastor Mitchell asked.

Chapter 23

"I see you've been at your church for six years," Gary said, switching gears to a less-sensitive topic.

"Yes, sir. Celebrated my sixth anniversary just this past Sunday in fact."

"Congratulations. Did you all do anything to celebrate?" Thoreau asked.

"Of course. Actually, every year the church takes a Sunday to celebrate my pastoral anniversary."

"*Every year*, huh?" Gary said for emphasis, looking at the rest of the team as if to say they needed to take notes.

"Oh yes. In the African-American church, the pastor's anniversary is a big deal. Every year."

"Aren't you worried that making such a big deal will create a kind of celebrity culture?" Jackson said.

"Not really. The Bible is clear that people like Dr. Kirkland and myself need to be honored. The apostle Paul said that those who preach the Word of God are worthy of double honor, and we see *honor* as not just a pat on the

142

back followed by, 'Good job.' We see it as rewarding a pastor with money. I'm not in the ministry for the material benefits, but I believe in being honored in material ways. Remember what Paul said to the congregation in 1 Corinthians 9:11: 'If we have sown spiritual things among you, is it too much if we reap material things from you?'"

"Curious, if you don't mind me asking," Janice cut in. "What did your church do for you at your anniversary?"

"They gave me a very generous financial gift and provided an all-expense paid vacation to Maui. It was their way of showing honor."

"Well, needless to say, we need to grow in that area," Janice said.

"Preach it, sister," Gary teased.

Pastor Mitchell laughed. "Whatever I can do to help my fellow pastor."

"Would you expect something similar at our church?" Janice asked delicately.

"Not to the same extent, because I would not be the senior pastor. However, as a leader, and one who teaches the Word, I would expect the first lady and me to be honored and appreciated by the flock."

"First lady?" Thoreau asked.

"That's what they call the pastor's wife in their church," Gary said.

Thoreau's expression betrayed his pessimism.

"Forgive me for asking," Janice said, "but it sounds like you have it really well at your church. Why would you even consider leaving an environment like that to come to our church—especially going from senior pastor to an associate position?"

"Good question, Sister Janice." Pastor Mitchell uncrossed his legs and leaned forward. "When I heard Dr. Kirkland share with our pastors' fellowship a while back that you wanted to take this church in a new direction, I felt God nudge my spirit. I look around at Greater Zion and I'm sure God is doing a great work in our church, but I also realize it's not a reflection of what the kingdom is to look like. And if I could be used by God to be part of something that looks more like heaven, you know multiethnic, then that's what I'd love to do. I'll still be preaching the Word. I'll be bringing in African Americans—but without the pressures of being the senior pastor." He nodded respectfully to Gary. "You want to make this congregation multiethnic. I know that I can help you make that happen. *That's* why I'm here."

Chapter 24

I want to be respectful of your time," Jackson said.

"You're fine, Mr. Chairman," Pastor Mitchell responded.

"I do have one last question for you. What's your relationship like with the elder board at your church?"

"Oh, we have some wonderful men at Greater Zion, really seasoned saints. I've been blessed. These men take the vision God has given me and they run with it."

Jackson furrowed his brow. "How do you reach a compromise? For instance, when they don't agree with something you want to initiate?"

"That doesn't happen." Pastor Mitchell raised his hands gently. "Let me explain. In the first year or two of my ministry, they gave me a bit of pushback, but that was to be expected. We were just getting to know one another after all. But then we clarified everyone's role."

"So no pushback?" Thoreau asked amazed.

"At all?" Wilson added.

"No," Pastor Mitchell said, shaking his head. "As I study

the Bible I don't see any case for a collaborative, or what some might call an *egalitarian* approach to leadership—"

"You mean," Janice interrupted, "where the team gets in a room and collectively figures things out."

"Yes. But that's not how we operate at Greater Zion." He looked at Gary. "I assume you . . .?"

Before Gary could respond, Jackson broke in. "How *do* you operate?"

"God tells me and I tell the people," Pastor Mitchell responded in a gracious but resolute way.

As soon as Pastor Mitchell's words hit the air, Peter knew this would shock every team member's ear in the room. Throughout Poplar Bible's history no one had led like this and remained to talk about it. That kind of "renegade" approach to leadership would have landed a pastor out of a job faster than he could have found Genesis 1:1 in a Bible sword drill. Poplar Bible was a well-oiled machine, maintaining a complex system of checks and balances that ensured pastoral accountability. In political speak, while Poplar Bible was a democracy, Greater Zion was a benevolent dictatorship.

"What's your biblical precedent for your leadership philosophy?" Thoreau asked.

"Moses on Mount Sinai when he received the Ten Commandments and gave them to the people. The Old

Testament prophet who heard a word from the Lord and spoke that word to the community. Jesus with the twelve disciples. I don't think there was much collaboration going on there," Pastor Mitchell answered with his first touch of gentle sarcasm.

"Yes, but what about Paul's instructions to Timothy and Titus about the need to set up elders? Doesn't that assume collaboration?" Jackson responded.

"That's your perspective seen through your cultural lenses. The way I look at those passages is that I begin with the question, '*Whom* was Paul writing to?'"

"Timothy and Titus," Jackson said.

"And what were their roles in the church?"

"They were the pastors."

"Exactly. So here you have an apostle, having received a word from God, telling local church pastors how to set up their elder board. The way I read it is that the elders were responding to the visionary of the house, which is the senior pastor. Paul's not writing to a collective body of men telling them to figure out their leadership structure. It's the pastor who has received a vision from God through an apostle, now telling other men, 'Here's what's going to happen.' Nothing in the text suggests that Timothy was like, 'Hey, guys, I got this idea about having elders. What do you think? And oh, let's vote on it.' Again, I'm not trying to offend. I'm just offering my cultural view." And with that Pastor Mitchell reached for the bottle of water sitting in front of him.

"Are there any other questions for Pastor Mitchell?" Gary asked. When no one commented, Gary rose, followed by the rest of the group, thanked Pastor Mitchell, and escorted him from the room.

Chapter 25

Wasting no time, Peter rolled up his sleeves and moved to the whiteboard. "So what did you think of Pastor Mitchell?"

The team was quiet for a moment. Peter sensed they were trying to form the appropriate words.

"Great guy," Thoreau finally said, while the group nodded in affirmation. "Interesting guy. . . . He's just not *our* guy."

"Why do you say that?" Peter asked.

"Well, I don't think his philosophy of leadership would work here," Thoreau answered.

"I agree," Janice said. "His view of elders is just unbiblical, to be honest."

"How so?"

"His whole bit about God telling him and then he tells the people sounds slightly cultish. A little weird."

"Okay. Could it be that it's just different?" Peter asked. "Can you be a Christian and have a different philosophy of leadership or church governance?"

"I guess so," Thoreau said reluctantly.

Janice peered at Peter over the edge of her glasses, looking perplexed.

"Don't tell me *you* think this is our guy?" Jackson asked incredulously.

Peter wanted to see how much they'd learned from his discussion about the different cultures. "Maybe, maybe not," Peter said with a grin as he watched Jackson's mouth drop slightly. "What else stood out to you about Pastor Mitchell?"

"It wasn't one thing for me," Wilson said. "It was a lot of little things."

"Like what?" Peter asked.

"Okay, call me an old fogey, but his gangster-looking suit and blue alligator shoes were just inappropriate."

Peter picked up the black dry-erase marker and wrote, "Alligator shoes/Gangster suit" on the whiteboard. Then he turned back to Wilson. "What else weirded you out?"

"They call him 'Pastor Mitchell' thing."

Peter wrote, "Pastor Mitchell" on the board as Wilson talked.

"And then the fact that his preaching style had this singing thing at the end of his messages. That's really foreign to our people."

"Preaching style," Peter repeated as he wrote the words

on the board. "This is good, keep going."

Wilson picked up Pastor Mitchell's resume and looked at it. "Nothing on his educational resume suggests that he has related to, or knows how to relate to, whites," he said.

"*Yes!*" Peter practically yelled as he slammed down the marker, and marched over to Wilson to give him a hug. The shock of Peter's action made Wilson sit back in his chair and pat his chest. Then he began to laugh a deep, understanding laugh.

"Pastor Mitchell went to all black schools," Peter said, standing next to Wilson's chair. "Nothing's wrong with that per se, but what this job requires is not just competence, but the ability to relate to different cultures. I don't see it on his resume, do you?" He could see the team was starting to get it now. They all sat straighter in their chairs or leaned in toward Peter. Their faces showed an openness and enthusiasm for the discussion.

"Look at the board," Peter said. He turned toward the whiteboard and began to read the words he'd listed there.

Alligator shoes/Gangster suit
"Pastor Mitchell"
Preaching style
Leadership style
Black schools

"Now, hear me on this, team, none of these items is right or wrong. In fact they're all cultural. The way Pastor Mitchell is addressed, preaches, leads, and even what he wears is a home run in his urban culture. But they are huge disconnects here at Poplar Bible."

"Yeah, Pete, but this seems so petty to say that someone's not the right guy because the *way* he preaches or leads is culturally different," Jackson said confused.

"I totally see and agree with your point, but this isn't ultimately why I believe Pastor Mitchell is not our guy. Remember when you and he were talking about preaching style?"

Jackson nodded.

"And you told him that you had hesitations about him being a good preaching fit stylistically? What was his response; do you remember?"

"Yes, he shot back and wondered if we were trying to make him white."

"Yes!" Peter said. "That's the problem, Jackson. It's not that he's culturally different, it's that he's *culturally inflexible*. Pastor Mitchell is what we would call a C3. C3s are people who are firmly entrenched in their ethnicity and culture and refuse to assimilate or adjust to another culture or ethnicity. They are who they are, and they're not going to change. Pastor Mitchell is not our guy because he's culturally different; he's just not our guy because the job demands that he make cultural adjustments. Not only does he refuse, but I'm not sure he even knows how. It's like Wilson said, nothing in his resume shows us that he can culturally adjust to whites. He didn't go to school with them. He doesn't live with them, and they don't come to his church or serve on his leadership teams.

"But there's something else about C3s you need to know. They typically see the world through their cultural lens, which means to them, their perspective is right and everyone else's tends to be wrong."

"Like Ice Cube? Is he a C3?" Thoreau asked.

"Yes, you could say that," Peter answered. "Ice Cube has a definite view about his people and culture. And he has no interest in being dissuaded from that. Good."

"Is there an example of a C3 in the Bible?" Wilson asked.

"Of course. The Pharisees are classic C3s. Remember when we read that passage in Philippians 3 where Paul said that he was a Hebrew of Hebrews? That was C3 language. Before his conversion, Paul was a Pharisee, and the Pharisees were always at odds with Jesus. Much of the conflict centered over the Pharisees' refusal to culturally adjust. So they berated Jesus for letting His disciples pick grain on the Sabbath. They went to war with Jesus for healing on the Sabbath, or not forcing His disciples to wash their hands before they ate. They went crazy over the fact that Jesus ate with prostitutes and tax collectors—a big cultural no-no. In each case Jesus revealed that these were cultural practices and preferences, not essential requirements. You can always spot a C3—they hold on to their cultural preferences and norms as if it's gospel truth."

Peter paused, letting his explanation sink in. "By the way," Peter said, breaking the silence. "Pastor Mitchell wasn't the only C3 in this room."

Chapter 26

I'm not sure what you mean by that, Pete," Jackson said.

"It's interesting that whenever I talk about C1s, C2s, and C3s, the automatic assumption is that I'm only talking about minority groups like African Americans or Hispanics, but this also includes whites. For example, have you ever met a white person who struck you as a person who 'acted black'?"

"Oh yeah, sure," Thoreau said.

"Give me an example."

"In the entertainment world I naturally think of the hip-hop artist Eminem," Thoreau said.

"You all are experts at this!" Peter said.

"Never heard of the guy," Wilson said. "You got some of his music on your phone? Play his music for us, Peter."

Thoreau and Peter immediately started to laugh.

"Wouldn't be appropriate, Wilson," Peter said.

"But Eminem would be a great example of a C1, a white guy ethnically who has assimilated into black culture.

But now let's talk about C3s. Give me an example."

"Me," Jackson said reluctantly.

"Interesting. Why do you say you're a C3?" Peter asked.

"Well, like Pastor Mitchell, I don't really have meaningful experiences or ongoing relationships with people of different ethnicities. And that whole deal about C3s seeing things from their cultural perspective and assuming their way is right—man, that nailed me right between the eyes. I just assume the style of Bible teaching or music or the way we do church here is the default. I'm forty-two and stuck in my cultural ways, I'm ashamed to say."

Jackson's vulnerability caught the room off guard, interjecting a pause in the conversation. Peter looked at Jackson with great affection, placing his hand on his shoulder.

"Proud of you," Peter said, whispering in Jackson's ear. Then moving back to the whiteboard, Peter continued his lesson. "This is so key for us to understand. When Pastor Mitchell walked into the room, I felt suspicion and a little judgment coming from you. This only heightened as the interview went on, and if I'm honest, I think it's because he didn't fit your cultural way of doing things. From the clothes, to the way he preaches, to the fact that he has an annual pastoral anniversary—all of this was met with judgment, because you all assume, and I say this gently, that your way of doing things is the right way."

Janice looked down at her hands, hiding her eyes.

Peter knew this was difficult for the group to hear, but he wanted to make sure they didn't hide or escape from the truth—since he knew ultimately the truth could set them free to truly pursue the multiethnic trajectory.

"Let's take pastoral anniversaries and his title," he continued. "The black experience is one of honor. We are taught to esteem the older and those who are in leadership positions. In traditional black culture this means that we don't call adults, or those in high positions, by their first name; we call them by some title. In the black experience the pastor is as high as it gets. Back in the day it was an honor for him to come to your house and eat—so much so that he was served before the women and children. We honor. Whites not so much."

"That's not completely true, though, Peter," Wilson said.

"He's right, Pete," Jackson said. "Southerners are polite and use titles with their elders."

"I think it's more of a generational thing with whites, though," Janice admitted, finally looking up. "We're becoming less and less formal."

"That's true. It's common to see white kids call adults by their first names." Peter pointed at Gary. "Dr. Kirkland here is not Dr. Kirkland, he's just Gary. But no matter what generation, in the traditional black church we would never call him Gary. Did you notice that Pastor Mitchell was put off when you called Gary by his first name? Not a right or wrong thing, just a cultural difference. Who's right? Who's wrong?" Before anyone could answer, Peter continued, "I don't think it's a matter of right or wrong. Now if that's the case, why does Pastor Mitchell have to adjust to you? Why not adjust to him and his way of doing things? See, if you put two C3s together of different ethnicities, you're going to have an explosion because neither side is going to give. That's why Pastor Mitchell couldn't work here. It's not only because he won't budge, it's also because you won't give either. Isn't it ironic that you all are as stuck in your ways as he is in his?"

Chapter 27

"B ut I never see myself as being white," Janice said sincerely.

"I know, and I believe you, Janice," Peter said. "In fact, I believe most white people don't see themselves as being white. And this is a huge disconnect in our society, because minorities are constantly in tune with their ethnicity, while you're not in tune with yours. It would be like me pointing out to you that you have two arms. You'd shrug as if to say, *Big deal*. You don't see yourself as having two arms, and neither do you see yourself as being white. But now imagine I had only one arm, and was constantly made aware that I was different in a two-arm society. If we're going to get along, you're going to have to understand what life is like for me having only one arm. That's the disconnect between whites and minorities. We live in a white world—a two-armed society, so to speak—but we minorities have only one arm. Life as a minority can feel like you're handicapped at times when compared to our white brothers and sisters."

"I see what you're saying," Thoreau said. "I've grown up with a lot of privileges, and there's not a day that goes by when I don't stop and realize how blessed I am. I also know that I have to steward my blessings well. So if what you're saying is true, why not hire a guy like Pastor Mitchell and put us in a position where we have to adjust to him? Don't you think that would be healthy?"

"In an ideal world it would be," Peter admitted. "But we don't live in an ideal world. And remember, Poplar Bible is composed primarily of C3s who are used to doing life their way. Not only that, but they've attended a church who has affirmed their cultural worldview for the last forty years. Bring in Pastor Mitchell now and the C3s will simply revolt, either leaving or forcing him out. I've seen this happen too many times, right, Gary?"

Gary nodded, abandoning his usual smile.

"Okay, I'm putting this together," Jackson said, as though he were making his final argument before a jury. "Ronald was too safe. He is a C1, like Carlton Banks. Hiring him would be like hiring another one of us." He gestured to the whole team. "Whereas Octavius is at the other extreme, so different from us and unwilling to change that he would cause an explosion in our church—because C3s can't lead C3s of a different ethnicity. Is that right, Pete?"

"My man!" Peter exclaimed, slapping high five with Jackson.

"So if C1s are too safe, and C3s too divisive, then by process of elimination we need a C2," Jackson said, now pleased with himself. "But what exactly is a C2?"

"I'm glad you asked."

Part 6

Denzel

Chapter 28

Peter picked up his briefcase from next to his chair and placed it on the table. He shuffled through the contents until he found a magazine and pulled it out. On the cover was a large portrait shot of Denzel Washington. He plopped it on the table in front of the team.

"Tell me, what do you think of this guy?" he asked.

"Oh, I just love him," Janice exhaled, taking off her glasses. "If anything ever happened to my husband . . ."

"TMI, Janice, TMI," Jackson said in a jovial way.

"Great actor. Probably the best actor of our time," Thoreau chimed in.

"What are some of your favorite Denzel Washington films?" Peter asked, as he returned to the whiteboard.

"*Glory*," Gary said.

"*Glory*," Peter repeated, writing the word on the board.

"*Training Day*. After all, he did win the Oscar for that one," Janice said.

"I believe he won an Oscar for *Glory* as well," Peter said, and wrote, "*Training Day.*"

"*Out of Time*," Jackson said. "*Flight*—"

"*The Bone Collector*," Gary said.

"Ooh, that was a good one," Janice said.

With each movie title the team yelled out, Peter tried to keep up, writing each one on the whiteboard. "Okay, I think we have enough here." He stood back and studied the list.

Glory
Training Day
Out of Time
Flight
The Bone Collector
Malcolm X
The Taking of Pelham 123

Next he turned to the team. "Talk to me about this list. What does it say about Denzel Washington?"

"I just think of the incredible range of roles this guy can play," Thoreau said.

"Yes, good. Keep going."

"I mean, in *Training Day* he's really a street thug with a badge, but in *The Bone Collector* he's a paralyzed cop who helps thwart a serial killer," Thoreau continued.

"And who can forget that scene in *Glory* where Denzel's character gets beaten as if he's some slave?" Wilson said.

"Powerful scene, Wilson. Here's what I want us to do. Identify each of his movie characters with the C1, C2, C3 traits. What do you see?"

The team studied the list for a few moments, then Jackson broke the ice. "Well, Malcolm X is definitely a C3 role. I mean here was a guy who refused to adjust or change. You talk about someone who dug his heels in."

Peter wrote "C3" next to *Malcolm X*.

"And I'd have to say Denzel's role in *Glory* was a C3 role," Wilson said. "In fact he was making fun of that other black guy in the film for coming across as white. What did he call him? 'Snowflake,' I think?"

Peter wrote "C3" next to *Glory*.

"In *Flight* I could see that being a C1 role," Janice added. "I mean, really, it's an ethnically neutral role; anyone could play the pilot he played."

Thoreau nodded. "Same for *The Bone Collector* and *The Taking of Pelham 123*."

When they had finished their discussion, Peter again stood back so they could all survey the results.

Glory C3
Training Day C3
Out of Time C1
Flight C1
The Bone Collector C1
Malcolm X C3
The Taking of Pelham 123 C1

Peter quietly let the list with the cultural designations sink in.

After a few moments, Janice spoke up. "Wow, I've never looked at Denzel like this before."

"How could you, Janice? I mean I don't think you really were too concerned about his acting abilities—if you know what I mean," Jackson said, having a little fun.

"No, I'm serious," Janice said. "I go back to Thoreau's word that he used—*range*. It's pretty incredible how Denzel can go back and forth like this."

"I think you all know where I'm going with this," Peter said and moved back to his seat. "Denzel Washington is what we would call a C2. C2s are people who have the unique ability to go from one culture to another, without compromising or losing who they are in the process. Denzel is just as much Denzel in *Malcolm X*, as he was in *The Bone Collector*. After all, Denzel is able to command top dollar for the films that he stars in because people know that no matter what role he plays they're going to always get Denzel Washington. He is a C2.

"And my contention is that leaders at the highest levels of organizations, companies, and churches who are trying to move that entity in a multiethnic direction *have* to be C2. And yes, Wilson, I know what you're going to ask. We see this all throughout the Bible."

Chapter 29

I want you to think of God as a CEO, and the company He has founded is the church. God's goal is ambitious—He wants to create a place, which among other things, is multi-ethnic," Peter explained. "It's a place where Jews and Gentiles can come alongside one another and do life together. In order for this to happen, his 'executives' of the church have to be C2-type leaders. But these men were Jews who had little to no experience with Gentiles. So what did God do? Well, in Acts 10, God had Peter, a Jew, live in the home of a man named Simon the tanner. Now this was really uncomfortable for Peter because as a tanner, Simon's job was to work with dead animals—a huge cultural no-no to Jews. Since committed Jews like Peter would never work with dead animals—a job most common among Gentiles—that means Simon was probably a Gentile. So Peter had to be uncomfortable staying in the home of a Gentile. But that wasn't all. Later on in Acts 10 Peter had a vision in which a sheet filled with non-kosher items was placed in front of him and God told him to eat. After some initial resistance, God reprimanded Peter, and let him know that all that He has created is clean. Peter had the green light as a Jew to eat some ribs, with Memphis's famous dry rub on them, of course."

The team laughed.

"Finally, the Holy Spirit led Peter to go to the home of *another Gentile* named Cornelius, where he preached the gospel to a house full of Gentiles. The Holy Spirit moved and they gave their lives to Christ. A Jew did life with some Gentiles, and the church began to take shape. Notice that God didn't just put Peter, a Jew, in a room full of Gentiles and *bam* the church began. No, God first gave Peter a set of cultural experiences that prepared him for his role. But—and this is really important, team—in order for Peter to get these new cultural experiences, he had to be willing to immerse himself in uncomfortable places, places that were out of the cultural norm for him. Have you all had any experiences like this?"

"I went to an African-American church once," Thoreau said.

"Once, huh?" Peter asked, somewhat sarcastically, then smiled.

"Yeah, I felt really out of place for like the first time in my life."

"Good, now you get a little glimpse of how most minorities feel every day of their lives when they have to go to schools or jobs where they are surrounded by whites." Peter looked at the others in the room. "Any other experiences?"

The team was deep in thought, clearly trying to remember times when they were the minority. But they remained silent.

"Okay, let's go back to Paul. Remember we said he was a C3. We get this from what Paul wrote in Philippians 3 when he was talking about his life prior to Christ. Now look at what Paul said happened to him after he became a Christian. This is in 1 Corinthians 9:19–23." Peter picked up Gary's Bible, turned to the passage, and began to read aloud.

"For though I am free from all, I have made myself a servant to all, that I might win more of them. To the Jews I became as a Jew, in order to win Jews. To those under the law I became as one under the law (though not being myself under the law) that I might win those under the law. To those outside the law I became as one outside the law (not being outside the law of God but under the law of Christ) that I might win those outside the law. To the weak I became weak, that I might win the weak. I have become all things to all people, that by all means I might save some. I do it all for the sake of the gospel, that I may share with them in its blessings."

Peter placed the Bible back on the table. "Notice that Paul invited us into his circle of friendships, and who he did life with was very diverse. He said that he had some Jews for friends. But Paul also let us know that he had some Gentiles for friends. That's what he meant when he said, 'To those outside the law.' I mean, read the end of Paul's letters and the list of names he gave 'shout-outs' to. Have you ever stopped to think how diverse those names, and therefore his friendships, were? See, team, this 1 Corinthians 9 passage I just read to you is classic C2 language."

"Okay, I'm officially confused," Jackson said, putting his hands on his head. "I'm really trying to get this. I thought you said Paul was a C3, but now he's a C2?"

"That's right," Peter said, smiling.

"Remember, Paul described his life prior to Christ in Philippians 3 as being a C3—a Hebrew of Hebrews. But in 1 Corinthians 9, we're dealing with a different phase of his life, one that had been radically redirected by the gospel. And in this passage he said he was a C2. That's why Paul would say that he did all this for the sake of the gospel."

"So are you telling me someone can change their culture?" Jackson asked.

"That's exactly what I'm saying, Jackson." Peter walked behind Jackson and put his hands on Jackson's shoulders. "What I'm saying is that C2s are *made* and not born."

Chapter 30

"I'm confused like Jackson," Wilson said.

"Actually, if I follow what Peter is saying, this is really inspiring!" Thoreau clapped his hands together.

"Why?" Peter asked Thoreau.

"Well, because if you are born a C3, and you could never change that, then that's pretty deflating. It's like you're labeled something that you can't ever get out of. Who wants to stay stuck and not grow?" said Thoreau. "But if you can develop or morph into something else, something that's more effective and useful, then that's what *I* want to be about."

"Okay, I see what you're saying, Thoreau," Janice said. "I guess my question is how? How do you change from a C3 to a C2?"

"That *is* the question, isn't it?" Peter said and walked again to the whiteboard. "Believe it or not, the answer is right before your eyes. Look again at our 1 Corinthians 9 passage. In verse 22, Paul used three words." Peter picked up the marker and wrote the words, *I have become. I have become.* "These are very important words because what Paul was saying is that his ability to construct such an eclectic circle of friends was a learned skill, and the way that he learned it was by immersing himself into the social networks and environments of others. In fact, all throughout the passage Paul used the words, *I became.* To the Jew, Paul said, he *became* a Jew. To those outside the law—that would be Gentiles, by the way—he said, *I became.* You don't become a C2 by reading a book, or sitting in a nice conference room like this one hearing about it. No, the way C2s are made is when an individual immerses themselves into the environments and lives of people who are different from them. And *this* is where I believe our white friends are severely handicapped compared to minorities."

"What are you saying, Pete?" asked Jackson.

"Think about it, Jackson, in order for you to be successful in America, you don't have to learn how to relate to minorities. You can go to white schools, live in white communities, attend white churches, and play golf at white country clubs—that won't let my people in—and do just fine. Just look at you. Great job, great family. You've done pretty well for yourself.

"But show me any minority who's achieved success by our world's standards—you know, is making six figures, well educated, lives in a great neighborhood—and I promise you that person has learned the art of *I have become*. Minorities don't get their slice of the American pie without learning how to relate to our white brothers and sisters. We *have* to become. It's a matter of survival—those who don't get passed by. But what's sad is that this isn't a two-way street. Whites can totally ignore people like me and do just fine. I think this is what Ralph Ellison was pointing to in his book *Invisible Man*."

Peter could hear the passion in his voice. He wasn't bitter about the reality of what he was saying; he was excited that he had the opportunity to share this knowledge with a group of his brothers and sisters in Christ who truly wanted to learn.

"But what's sad for you is that in the process of ignoring me and my people, your C3 muscles are only strengthened, and your ability to become C2 atrophies," Peter continued. "On the other hand, we minorities who have experienced some measure of success have become C2s along the way."

Peter looked at Thoreau. "You asked a great question when you wanted to know how someone becomes a C2, but the greater question is *why*? Why would someone want to go through the trouble of getting into the shoes of another culture? Why would anyone want to embrace discomfort willingly? Anyone want to give it a shot?"

"Well," Wilson offered, "if I'm looking at this passage, I guess I'd have to say what Paul says in verse 23: 'I do it all for the sake of the gospel.'"

"Yes!" Peter shouted, and just as he was about to run to Wilson to hug him again, Wilson smiled and put his arms up to shield himself.

"Okay, I won't hug you again, Wilson. But you nailed it! Paul said he went through all the discomfort of *I have become* for the sake of the gospel. Paul's friendships were diverse because the gospel was diverse. Jesus didn't just die for black people or white people or Asians or Hispanics, He died for the *world*! The gospel is diverse, so therefore our friendships should be diverse.

"Not only that, but the gospel came to be through the discomfort of the cross. Jesus willingly submitted Himself to the uncomfortable so that we could be adopted into the eclectic family of God. If this is true, then being the only white in a three-hour, African-American service is really a small price to pay, don't you think, Thoreau?" Peter said, smiling.

Thoreau nodded in agreement.

"So what was the result of Paul morphing into a C2? The multiethnic church was formed. Like Gary shared with us, Paul could walk into the synagogue one day, and be surrounded by Greek philosophers on Mars Hill the next. Classic C2! Multiethnic churches and movements *have* to have C2 leadership at the top."

"I get what you're saying, Peter," Thoreau said. "But how do we spot a C2 during the interview process?"

"Yes, great question, Thoreau. This piece of paper says a lot more than what you think." Peter held up a resume. "Don't just look for degrees or GPAs. Try to discern if there are any C2 indicator lights."

"But what does that mean?" Janice asked.

"Look for things like the ethnic makeup of the candidate's school. Was it all black like Pastor Mitchell's? Check out the fraternities he pledged, the ethnic demographics of the churches he's worked at, or the extracurricular activities he's a part of. Most important, don't get hung up on one piece of his social matrix; see if all the pieces fit together to form a diverse picture."

"Keep talking some more about this," Janice said, as she picked up her pen and started to take notes.

"Probe into his friendships. Who a guy hangs out with does a lot to form who he is socially, and is a huge indicator of where he falls on the cultural grid. Most important, you want to see how he handles himself in situations where he is the minority. Does he adjust his preaching style, tone down his dress, tighten up his language? Remember, we're not asking a guy to change who he is, we're simply asking him to make some cultural adjustments that are appropriate to his context. C2s have learned to do this to the point where it eventually becomes second nature to them."

"What do you mean, 'tighten up his language'?" Jackson asked.

"Yeah, great question," Peter said, inwardly amused. "Okay, C2s are bilingual even if English is the only language they speak."

Jackson offered a blank look.

"There's a way we as minorities talk to each other when it's just us in the room that's different when we're around you all."

"I knew that African Americans talked differently among themselves, Pete, but you do that too?" Jackson asked.

"I am African American, Jackson. It's just a side to me that you haven't seen."

"Come on, Peter, show us the side," Thoreau said playfully.

"Yeah, Peter, come on and show us," Janice said.

"I'm good," Peter said, laughing out loud.

When the laughter died down, Jackson pressed on. "But I still don't feel like I could spot a C2, especially when I've realized I'm a C3. Do you get what I'm saying, Pete?"

"Yes, which is why the number one rule in hiring a

minority is that there has to be a person on the team who represents the demographic you're going after. In other words if you're looking to hire someone who's Chinese, you need a Chinese person on the search committee.

"I'll give you an example. Some years ago when I was leading a church in Birmingham, our team was looking to expand our efforts into the Hispanic community. I remember one meeting when we got to talking about whether or not we wanted to reach first- or second-generation Hispanics. Now this is a big deal because first generation typically doesn't speak English. So if we were going to go after first generations, we'd have to inject some discomfort into our services by making them bilingual. As you can imagine this was a huge talking point. Back and forth we went, until I had an epiphany. Why were we trying to figure out the best way to reach the Hispanic community with no Hispanics on our team to help guide the discussion? I put the brakes on our meeting until we could find someone to help lead us. Never hire a person of a different ethnicity without someone of that ethnicity in the room during the interview. As the old saying goes, it takes one to know one."

Chapter 31

T his has been really helpful, Peter," Gary said, now inserting himself into the discussion. "Could you talk
some about how exactly a C2, African-American leader
would help us here at the church?"

"Sure. Remember, C2s are highly intuitive people, who
remain who they are but adjust cultural preferences and
norms to nudge the people in the direction where things
need to go. C2s don't berate the people and demand that
they go in a certain direction. Instead they have a keen
cultural awareness of what needs to happen to move from
point A to point B in the journey toward multiethnicity.

"Take Jesus, for example, the ultimate C2 leader. He
could've looked at His tribe of Jewish followers on their
first day together and said, 'All right, boys, the kingdom of
God demands we hang around the Gentiles, so Peter you
go stay at Simon the tanner's house right now. Get with the
program. I said it, you do it.' Jesus didn't do that. Instead
He took small steps—like a day trip to Samaria, healing

missions into Gentile territory, and brief encounters with people like the Canaanite woman. He knew His Jewish followers had to become C2, multiethnic leaders, but He also knew their development wouldn't happen overnight, so instead He provided small but significant opportunities that put them just outside their comfort zones. Jesus nudged, He didn't push. But Jesus didn't sell out either. He didn't say, 'You know these Jews have some pretty biased opinions, and I need them to think well of Me so I'll just leave it alone, and not even deal with issues of race.' No, He didn't do that."

Peter really felt as though the group was getting his explanation. He picked up his bottle of water, took a swig, and then continued.

"A C2 leader here at Poplar Bible is going to realize that the music isn't what it should be, but he's not going to go out and hire Kirk Franklin, or some heavy gospel artist who will jolt the church into pandemonium. But neither will he hire some safe, Maranatha praise band that only offers more of the same. He's going to look to provide an experience that will gently nudge you out of your comfort zone, instead of jolting you out of the church.

"A C2 leader is going to look at this staff and realize that the leadership community is nowhere near where it should be in its ethnic and cultural makeup. He knows some changes need to be made, but he also knows those changes won't come overnight. He'll gently and methodically build up relational capital with the powers that be and make the strategic hires necessary. He'll also know he can't make all or even the majority of his hires black, but he'll be sure to keep a great balance.

"The primary place where you'll feel the weight of a C2 around here is in the pulpit. A great C2 leader will understand two things when it comes to his preaching. One, that he has to address issues of race and diversity because that's what the Bible addresses and it's strategic to the new vision and mission of this church. And two, he'll know that his responsibility is to not turn the pulpit into a sociological platform, but to always be faithful to the text and the gospel of our Lord and Savior Jesus Christ. The effective C2 preacher talks infinitely more about Jesus Christ than he does race and ethnicity. In fact, any remarks on race, a C2 leader will connect to the gospel of Jesus Christ."

"Amen!" Wilson shouted.

Suddenly the door to the conference room opened and Gary's assistant stepped in, alerting the team that the next candidate had just arrived.

"So tell us about this candidate, Jackson," Gary said.

Jackson pushed the resume away from in front of him. "Based on what I'm hearing, I don't think he even needs to come in the room."

Chapter 32

What do you mean, he doesn't need to come in the room?" Janice dropped her pen onto her notepad and looked sharply over her glasses at Jackson.

"Are you saying that we don't need to interview him?" Thoreau asked. "I mean, look at his resume, it's pretty impress—"

"He's not our guy," Jackson cut in.

"And I see a bunch of what Peter calls, 'C2 indicator lights,'" Janice replied, ignoring Jackson.

"He was an English major at the University of Tennessee, where he also pledged an African-American fraternity," Thoreau said.

"Yeah," Janice continued, "and he went to Dallas Theological Seminary, which is a primarily white school, but I see here that he served on the staff of an all-black church in the inner city of Dallas."

Jackson merely shook his head as Thoreau and Janice

pleaded with him. "I'm telling you, this guy's not worth bringing in the room."

Peter agreed with Janice and Thoreau's assessment, based solely on the resume, so he was surprised by how hard Jackson was digging in his heels. What was he up to?

"Don't you see that he's served the last several years as a teaching pastor at a multiethnic church in Greenville, South Carolina?" Thoreau continued.

"And everyone, both white and black, went on and on about his preaching," Janice said.

Jackson was still not convinced. "Guys, you're going to have to trust me on this one. He's not who we want to serve as a teaching pastor here at Poplar Bible."

Janice slammed the candidate's resume onto the conference room table and stood. Her face had turned a bright red. "I know what this is, and I had a hunch you'd do this, *Jackson Rush*. You're sabotaging this whole process because you want a white guy in this position. Admit it! Just say it, Jackson—you're a *bigot*!"

"Whoa, there, Janice!" Wilson said, raising both hands in an attempt to calm her. "This is not the way we conduct ourselves as Christians, much less as leaders in this church."

Janice was not to be appeased. Her jaw set tensely and her hands fisted up.

Gary stood and clapped his hands to get everyone's

attention. "It's been a long day, team. Maybe we should call it quits, gather ourselves, and reengage this at a later time."

Gary's assistant, still standing next to the door, cleared her throat. "Do you want me to send him in?" she whispered, in an unsure tone.

"No," Jackson said.

"Yes," Janice and Thoreau demanded at the same time.

Gary's assistant looked at him for help.

Gary sighed and rubbed his chin thoughtfully. "I think we need to defer to the chairman. Give us a few moments."

She swallowed hard and nodded, then quickly exited the room.

As soon as the door closed behind her, Jackson stood and inhaled and exhaled slowly, as though he were gathering all the composure he could. "I have no doubt Roderick would make a fine addition to our staff. The candidate's name is Roderick, isn't it?"

Peter looked at the resume. "Yes."

"Thanks, Pete. But we're not tasked to make a great hire. We have to make the best possible hire there is. I'm just saying that I'm not convinced that Roderick is the best person for this position. And contrary to what some would say, this has nothing to do with me being a bigot." Jackson shot Janice a hard look. "I'm a lot of things. Call me misinformed, ignorant, naïve, but don't call me a bigot, especially after the last couple of weeks I've spent with this man." Still staring at Janice, he pointed directly at Peter.

"This whole ethnicity and culture thing has messed me up, as I'm sure it has all of us," Jackson continued. "I had no clue. I thought black was black and white was white, to be quite honest with you. Sure, I used the term *culture*, but I always thought of it as a synonym for ethnicity and vice versa. C1, C2, C3? I had no idea. But it's all making sense to me, it really is."

Jackson paced back and forth as he talked, giving the appearance that he was reaching for concepts and trying to understand what he was saying. Meanwhile, the team hung curiously and suspiciously onto every word, as though waiting anxiously for some punch line.

"I think in pictures, and you painted a great one for me that night at the ball game, Pete. Remember you told me about Branch Rickey and Jackie Robinson, and how if this whole plan of integrating the Negro Leagues was going to work, then Branch Rickey didn't have the luxury of making a mistake on the first guy?"

Peter nodded and noticed Gary's curious look at him. He smiled slightly, eyebrows raised.

"Pete told me that this first African-American ball player had to have two things. He had to be competent. He had to have the ability to hit and field and get the job done. Well, Jackie did that. But he also had to have what you called the right culture. He was going to take a lot of abuse from white ball players, and he couldn't lash out and get angry. He had to be able to relate well as the only black with his white teammates and opponents. Well, Jackie did that. Competence and culture, that's what we're after. And just as these two things served Jackie, the Brooklyn Dodgers, and the Major Leagues well, they'll serve us well here at Poplar Bible too."

"We're all agreed on that, Jackson," Janice said, now slowly taking her seat. "And—"

"Well, the first two guys we interviewed were competent, I think, but not good cultural fits," Jackson said. "One was too safe, and the other would've destroyed our church because of his refusal to make cultural adjustments."

"And our refusal too," Thoreau said. "Remember, Jackson, we're C3s, just like Octavius."

"Absolutely. And I have no doubt Roderick would have done a really good job here, just from the looks of things. He comes highly recommended by Pete's firm, and he has the right cultural makeup, it seems. There's just one problem."

"What's that?" Peter asked.

"He's not the best guy for the job," Jackson said, now staring at Peter.

"How on earth would you know that?" Janice shot back at Jackson, the anger still lodged in her voice.

Peter agreed with Janice. "With all due respect, Jackson, if as you say you're new to this, how do you know he's not the best guy for the job?"

Jackson took a deep breath, took one step back from his chair, and locked his eyes on Peter. "Because he's not you."

Chapter 33

Every mouth dropped in the room, except for Jackson's, whose lips remained firmly set. Then immediately the board members' eyes grew bright. Their mouths drew up in huge smiles. Though the sun was starting to set outside Poplar Bible, Peter felt as if the room had grown ten times brighter.

"Oh. My. Yes!" Janice said. "Jackson Rush, you're brilliant!" Janice quickly went to Jackson and threw her arms around Jackson in a peace offering.

"From bigot to brilliant in a matter of moments," Jackson said sarcastically.

"And what's more is that Gary and Peter have worked together before, so we know that they can pull this off," Wilson said.

"Why didn't we think about this before? We could've saved ourselves a lot of time," Thoreau said.

While the team was hugging and high-fiving one another, Gary cleared his throat loudly enough to grab their attention. "Before we break out the champagne, don't you think we should hear from Peter?"

Peter's hand was firmly holding his chin, while his eyes were looking into nothing. Jackson's words had caught him completely by surprise.

"What do you have to say to this, Peter?" Wilson asked, breaking the silence.

Finally, Peter snapped out of his pondering and collected his thoughts. "There's a reason I'm consulting and no longer leading a church," he said with a smile.

"You've got to do this, Peter," Janice said. "It all lines up perfectly. The way you came in and inspired us. Not many people can walk into a room filled with white people set in their cultural preferences and move them, or as you would say, 'nudge' them out of their ways."

"Jackson is onto something," Thoreau said. He pointed at the magazine picture of Denzel lying on the table, then directed his hand to Peter. "The picture you painted of a C2 isn't just Denzel, it's you."

"Anyone who can have the kind of effect that you've had on Jackson, *definitely* deserves to be on this staff," Janice said.

"I've never reported to a black man in all my life," Wilson said, fighting back emotions. "But I'd follow your leadership."

"Me too," Jackson said. He stepped next to Gary and Peter and spoke directly to them. "As Wilson said, you two know and love each other. There's a special trust you have established. A lot of water under this bridge." He pointed between them. "What do you say about this, Gary?"

Gary smiled brightly and patted Peter on the back. "Nothing would bring me greater joy than to be reunited on staff with my friend."

Peter lifted his hand to indicate he needed a moment, then walked to a window and stared out at the school. The streetlights were beginning to come on, guiding the last wave of commuters to their homes. Joining the parade of lights was the Poplar Christian Academy sign, which had just lit up and was still flickering to life. Something drew him to that sign.

"Does any of this interest you at all, Pete?" Jackson asked.

"It does make me stop and think," Peter said, still reflecting on the school's sign. "I'd need time to think about it, and of course pray and talk with my wife. But before I go down this road and even begin to process it all, there's just one thing I'd need from you."

"Name it," Jackson said.

Peter turned from the window to the team. "Poplar Christian Academy."

"Pop—Poplar Academy?" Jackson asked, looking unsure.

"Yep," Peter said. "The move gets put off for at least a year until we turn over every rock to figure out how to get the school to stay put."

"Ha!" Janice clapped her hands.

"Why the school?" Wilson asked.

Peter thought about the ratio of black and white students he'd seen that first day while sitting with Gary in the booth at Perkins. He thought about the importance of an education and the power it provided for minority students to grow and help the world develop more C2s. He wondered how many opportunities would be lost if those black students lost this school in their neighborhood. He didn't want it to happen on his watch—if he agreed to take this position. He briefly shared his thoughts with the team.

"I hear what you're saying, Pete, but I just don't know about it." Jackson shook his head. "If we stayed, it would cost us a lot of money. We've already bought property and made agreements."

"It would cost you a lot more to leave," Peter shot back. "I know it's a lot to ask. But you all just asked me for something big, and I figured I'd return the favor. I guess we'd both have to consider making a sacrifice. But if you're not willing . . ."

"Oh no, we're willing, *aren't* we, Jackson?" Janice said, giving him a look.

"I sure can't have you going nuts on me again," Jackson said as he raised his hands in the air in his defense.

"Okay, Pete, we'll consider it. What do you say?" Jackson extended his hand toward Peter.

Chapter 34

Memphians often joke that the way to hell has a lay-over in Atlanta. This was true for Peter as he was due to leave early the next morning for home, with a stop in the capital of the Peach State. Jackson, "the mayor of Memphis," insisted on taking his friend Pete to the airport. So just as the sun was peeking its head over the horizon, Peter threw his bags in the back of Jackson's car, and the two made their way down Interstate 240 toward the Memphis International Airport.

Their conversation couldn't have been more different from that late afternoon chat at that "meat and three" several weeks before. There was no deep dialog over race on this day, just two men who were forging a friendship, chatting about the Memphis Grizzlies basketball team, family, and whether or not Peter would take the teaching pastor job at Poplar Bible. As they made their way to the airport, Peter silently hoped for heavy traffic so his visit could be extended with his new pal, Jackson. Although Peter was not normally given to sentimentality, this felt different. He was really going to miss Jackson.

What would become of Jackson Rush in the weeks and months to follow? Would he revert to the same man Peter encountered at The Commissary? Or would Jackson continue down the path of transformation, openness, and compassion? Only time would tell. It was ultimately in the Holy Spirit's wise and masterful hands—and in Jackson's heart. Whether or not Peter took the job, Jackson's fate rested in his commitment to immerse himself in the narratives of others, of people who were different from him. Peter knew that if Jackson did this, there would be hope for him and for Poplar Bible.

Afterword

Finding Denzel

Nothing of great value happens apart from competent, caring, humble, proactive leadership. I don't think there's a hint of overstatement when I say that the trajectory of our families, churches, organizations, and society rests squarely on the shoulders of leaders. Every time an organization hires a leader, they place their future in his or her hands.

If this feels weighty to you, it should. I know we at Fellowship Memphis felt the gravity (and still do) of leadership when we launched in the spring of 2003. Church planting is tough. Planting a multiethnic church is even tougher. If Fellowship Memphis was going to fly, God would have to breathe on our efforts and guide us to the right leaders. We have bombarded the throne room of heaven every time we've needed to add a new leader to our ministry. Along the way we learned some valuable lessons in finding the right kind of leaders to help us experience our vision of a gospel-centered, disciple-making, multiethnic church.

C2 Leadership

Within every ethnicity there exists at least three cultural expressions: C1s, C2s, and C3s. What I have tried to show in this book is that at the highest levels of any entity that longs to be multiethnic there has to be what I call C2 leadership. Now don't get me wrong, there is a place for C1s and C3s in your organization—they just have to be in what Jim Collins, in his book *Good to Great*, calls the right seat on the bus. So what are those seats?

C1s are people from one ethnicity who have assimilated into another. In the Bible they are the Hellenistic Jews of Acts 6. The very name *Hellenistic Jew* communicates both ethnicity and culture, for they were Jews who had assimilated into Greek culture. C1s are not what some would pejoratively call an "Uncle Tom" or a "sellout." In an African-American context they are no less black than anyone else, they have just adapted thoroughly and tend not to push the limit culturally or ethnically. They can be categorized as culturally safe. C1s have the capacity to be wonderful leaders in the right position, but in my experience, they usually aren't the ones stretching the organization to become more multiethnic.

I was out to lunch with a pastor of a prominent church who was looking to hire the first African-American pastor in their history. He had the foresight to acknowledge that while this was an exciting endeavor, it could also blow up in his face. He needed some help and asked me for guidance. The position he was looking to fill was that of a small-groups pastor. This leader would play a key role in the church, but would not be on the executive team. There was no preaching involved, just working with established teams, developing leaders, and writing curriculum. As you've probably already deduced, ethnicity is not a key factor in the day-to-day responsibilities of this position. But since he wanted a minority, I told him in so many words he needed Carlton Banks—someone who had a wealth of experience with majority ethnicity, and would not be rattled when an offensive remark was made. Carlton would feel right at home worshiping on Sundays, and immersing himself in the ethnicity and culture of their church. We found him his guy, and things have gone really well, so well that he came back to me and hired an African-American teaching pastor, a C2. I don't think the church would have been ready for Denzel if Carlton had not led the way.

On the other extreme are the C3s. The phrase that embodies a C3 is *culturally inflexible*. In the Bible your C3s are the Pharisees. We tend to think of them only in legalistic terms, and while this is true, they also represent the culturally rigid. The Pharisees not only kept the law, but they kept the traditions as well. In fact, lurking behind many of the notorious clashes between Jesus and them, was some cultural tradition of which they refused to negotiate (such as hand washing, eating with certain groups of people, and what did and did not constitute work).

C3s are not pharisaical villains. In fact it might surprise you to hear that I believe there's a place for C3s in your organization. For example, many churches are starting community development corporations that demand leadership who can pound the pavement and relate to a specific demographic. The person leading that initiative needs to carry a fair amount of street cred with the target audience. I have seen well-intentioned organizations, thinking solely of ethnicity, hire a C1 (who relates well to them) to do what amounts to be the job of a C3, and it has failed miserably.

Where C3s can get you into trouble is when they are placed in predicaments where they must lead C3s of a different ethnicity. For example, in my church many (not all) of our white members are C3s, where they went to schools, nurtured friendships, and lived in neighborhoods that were primarily homogenous. They don't see themselves as being white, but nonetheless have adapted a way of viewing the world, and navigating relationships, that for better or worse is fixed. I have seen an African-American C3 point out the shortcomings of a white C3's worldview, and let's just say it didn't go well, and progress was not made, because neither was willing to adjust.

What I have learned over the years is that C2 leadership is essential at the highest echelons of any organization if they want to be multiethnic. A C2 is a person who is *culturally flexible and adaptable without becoming ethnically ambiguous or hostile*. Paul pointed to this in 1 Corinthians 9:19–23 when he said that he had become all things to all people. Like Denzel Washington, a C2 has a wide range of relationships and can navigate various ethnicities and cultures while maintaining his unique identity all at once. C2s are typically classified by high levels of cultural intelligence and sensitivity. They not only are committed to nudging the organization forward in matters of ethnicity, but they also know the rate in which they need to push without alienating their constituency.

Our church, Fellowship Memphis, has become part of the 2.5 percent of multiethnic churches because we have been ruthlessly committed to finding and developing C2 leadership. You cannot occupy a position on our executive team unless you are a C2. It's just too valuable to our vision and mission to lower our standards.

Finding Denzel

The million dollar question now becomes how? How are we able to find Denzel, or C2 leadership? In my years of hiring C2 leadership I have found three fundamental things that have helped me in bringing the right leaders onto our team: finding the right cultural resume, diversifying the search team, and keeping a strong, good attitude.

Find the right cultural resume

The primary indicator light for a C2 is their social and relational resume. Pay careful attention to their educational background. What schools did they attend? What was the ethnic makeup of those schools? What were their experiences growing up? Does their employment history point to a hybrid leader (C2) who is used to going in and out of various cultures and ethnicities? Who are their friends? In many cases no one facet of their life will answer these questions in the affirmative, but when you zoom out and look at the totality of their experiences, it should point to a rich mosaic of involvements and relationships.

The primary currency of a leader is relational capital. How a person relates to others is really a matter of life or death when it comes to leadership, and unfortunately you can't earn a degree in people; it comes only over time.

In the world of multiethnic churches and organizations, people skills are even more of a premium, where the leader becomes a hybrid able to navigate various ethnicities well. The only way to diagnose a candidate's relational skills is his past and current networks of people and experiences.

Diversify the search team

I've made the rookie mistake of hiring someone from another ethnicity in the hopes that they will be a right fit on our team without including people on our search team from the ethnicity and culture I was looking to hire. Great leaders are confident people, and many times this is what bites them. I have to admit to myself that I am not Korean, for example. So why would I go out and look for a C2 Korean leader without any C2 Koreans on my search team? Makes no sense, right? There's just an intuition that people of the same ethnicity share, which allows them to sense if this person would be the right fit.

Now I know what you must be thinking: how do you find someone to sit on your search team who represents the people you are trying to reach, when you don't even know of anyone of that ethnicity? This is where a little heavy lifting is needed. Chances are someone on the existing search team has a coworker or a friend of a friend who represents that demographic. If this doesn't work, spend time getting to know people from that community since they are in close proximity to your church or organization. Be honest and vulnerable, inviting them into your circumstance, and ask for help. This will endear you to this individual, not only getting the information you are looking for, but gaining an ally in the process.

I remember working at a church that decided they wanted to expand their reach into the growing Hispanic community. So they chose a wonderfully godly and gifted Hispanic leader. The only problem was that the people they were looking to reach were Mexican, and this ethnic leader was from Argentina (which are two *very* different cultures). Needless to say this was a train wreck that took them literally half a decade to recover from. All of this could have been avoided if they had taken the time to lean into some of the leaders from the Mexican community in helping them with their search.

Keep a good attitude

Attitude is key for every leader. In this instance I'm not talking about attitude in general, but something more specific. Multiethnic ministry is difficult. You will have one group telling you you're pushing too hard, and another demanding that you move faster. Add to this the insensitive things that people say to one another (and even you), and if you're not careful you can become bitter, or lead out of festering racial wounds that have not quite healed. As one author has noted, those of us in the area of racial reconciliation serve as bridges, and bridges get stepped on.

There's no room for me to lead out of bitterness. I think that's why when Moses struck the rock instead of speaking to the rock, God said his time was up. His outburst of anger revealed a wounded heart that had infected his attitude. How can I lead a certain ethnicity and harbor suspicious feelings toward them? Because attitude is so important, when I interview a person who I believe is a C2, I will at some point place them in a room where everyone else is of a different ethnicity and watch very carefully how they respond. I want to discern if there's a genuine sense of love on his part toward them, or if the person is too guarded. I'll poke and prod into their lives asking about hurts they have experienced, and listen very carefully not just to their narrative, but how they rehearse those moments. Love, Jesus said, is the primary badge of what it means to follow Him. Multiply this times a hundred for those of us in leadership.

Pursuing the Dream

Hiring a C2 leader is not the finish line, it's really just the beginning. Because C2s are made and not born, we constantly need to develop our C2 muscles. Our teams at the church read and discuss books, take trips together in which we are culturally stretched, and even watch provocative films that give us a runway to share our stories and learn from one another.

If ethnic ignorance is bred in isolation, then growth happens through community. Some of our most meaningful moments have come as we have discussed the Trayvon Martin verdict and films like *12 Years a Slave*. Over the years my preaching has redemptively softened, and my heart toward people of other ethnicities has become more sensitized, all because I have been in the trenches, immersed in their lives. My white colleagues have also said that their resolve to pursue Christ-exalting diversity has stiffened because their stereotypes and presuppositions have been exposed due to meaningful relationships with people who don't look like them. The fruit of it all has been a body that is marching ever closer to experience what Korie Edwards calls *The Elusive Dream*. This is my hope for you and your organization as well. We will get there.

Acknowledgments

When I originally submitted my idea to Moody for a book that would encourage thinking and equip people interested in moving their organizations in a multiethnic trajectory, I had a lot of subjects I wanted to tackle. The people at Moody, on the other hand, nudged me to focus in on the specific topic of *culture and ethnicity*, and build a whole book around this theme. Throughout the process I've found myself grateful for people like Roslyn Jordan and her team for their prodding.

As always I'm thankful for my wife, Korie, my agent, Andrew Wolgemuth, and assistant, Danielle Ridley, who read the manuscript and offered hope and helpful feedback. I would also be mistaken not to remember my dear church, Fellowship Memphis, the flock I've had the pleasure of leading for more than a decade. Every concept in this book on multiethnic leadership has been forged during my tenure with these beloved people. My prayer is that I would have the joy of shepherding this people for decades to come.

My father is known to ask the question, "What makes you pound the table and weep?" For me, I want to give my life to seeing the multiethnic church become the new normal in our country. Currently only 2.5 percent of American churches are multiethnic. This has to change, and by God's grace it will. I'm honored to play a small role in seeing this change, and I hope what you hold in your hands will be of great service to you.